THE NUTCOMBE PAPERS

BY

KEN KELSEY

This is a work of fiction.
Any resemblance to events or individuals
living or dead is purely
coincidental.

All rights reserved.

©   K J Kelsey
kelsey@talk21.com

Cover design by Rebecca Bagley
www.bagleyart.com
bagleyart@startmail.com

Contents

Chapter		Page
	Foreword	1
1	Stephen's Stag Night	3
2	The Winning Ticket	14
3	Joyce the Verger	25
4	The Bigamist	36
5	Daniel Dowd	44
6	Sid's Revenge	52
7	The Water Crisis	57
8	Daisy Dimple	63
9	The Arsonist	76
10	The Quinquennial Convention	85
11	The County Bus Strike	98
12	Cowboys	113
13	Jennifer Grayson	124
14	The Nun's Tale	138
15	The Major	158

FOREWORD

When my father died unexpectedly at the age of 46, my widowed grandfather came to live with my mother and me. Before he retired he had been a newspaper reporter, and would spin me many yarns of his early years covering local stories for provincial newspapers. My fondest childhood memories are as a boy of eight or nine, listening to his tales.

Sometimes my mother would chide him. "You're filling the lad's head with nonsense again, father," she'd say, but she would smile as she spoke, and I noticed that she would often contrive to be within earshot, enjoying the tales as much as I did.

Once I was bold enough to contradict her. "They're not nonsense. They are all true, aren't they, grandpa?"

My grandfather waved his Daily Mail and answered, "As true as anything you'll read in a newspaper, my boy."

Some parts of his stories I didn't understand, usually parts which would make my mother laugh and say, "Father! The boy's not old enough for that sort of thing." I stored these fragments carefully away in my memory, in anticipation of their coming to fruition at a later date.

I was saddened when he died, for he had done so much to shape my character. After his funeral, I found that he had left me a package containing a dozen or more reporter's notebooks, several yellowed newspaper cuttings and a few dog-eared photographs. The pages of the notebooks were covered with manuscript, some in his handwriting, and some in shorthand.

It took me many months to transcribe his notes into plain text. As I was doing so I was astonished to find that they contained several references to people and events which had featured in the tales he had told me. Believing this was his intention in leaving me this material, I have reconstructed a few of his tales, drawing upon his notebooks and from what I could remember of what he had told me about the 1950s when he was a reporter on The Nutcombe & District Advertiser and later on the Nutchester Chronicle. I have had to take a fair amount of licence in filling in the dialogue and other gaps, but I am confident that I have faithfully reproduced the substance of his experiences.

Frank Simpson
Editor

STEPHEN'S STAG NIGHT

Stephen Grimshaw never did have a mother. That is to say, Emily Grimshaw, the sixteen year old girl who nurtured him from the day he was born, brought him up to believe that she was in fact his Auntie Emily. So Stephen never had a mother, just an aunt. He did, however, have several uncles who visited Emily during the afternoon or evening, some even staying the night. The generosity of these uncles enabled Emily to bring him up in relative comfort, but he, lacking a suitable male rôle-model unsurprisingly grew up to be a wayward lad, receiving many a clip round the ear from the local bobby. Only the intervention of Cllr. Whelks, another uncle, saved him from the more serious consequences of his escapades.

As he grew older and bigger many of his uncles became inhibited by his presence, and Emily began to notice a marked decrease in their avuncular visits which had a detrimental effect upon the household budget. When Stephen was nearing twenty she told him it was time for him to flee the nest, to find a nice girl to marry, preferably one with well-to-do parents. So Stephen, anxious to please his aunt, tipped his cap at Grace Fellowes, a lovely, well-brought-up young lady.

Mr and Mrs Fellowes had no doubts whatever about Stephen's true lineage and cautioned their daughter when she and Stephen started to walk out together.

"He's not good enough for you," warned her mother. "He's not a nice boy. He's only after one thing, so make sure you keep your hand on your ha'penny."

In time the young couple announced that they intended to get married, which alarmed Mrs Fellowes even more.

4

"Just because you're engaged doesn't mean you can let him have anything on account," she said. "You keep that until your wedding night. Remember poor Maudie Baxter that was. She let her Gregory have something on account and look what happened to her. She loved it at first. 'Ooh,' she enthused, 'I could eat it'. Trouble was, her Gregory loved it even more, so that by the time of their wedding night she wished she had. They went to Torquay for their honeymoon but she said the only difference was the wallpaper in the bedroom. So you keep it 'til you're married, my girl."

Grace heeded her mother's advice, much to Stephen's disappointment, and the day of the wedding approached. Mr Fellowes was relatively well off and spared nothing in the preparations for his daughter's day at church. He was lavish in his expenditure and generous in his invitations, so much so that the Rev. Cornelius Sprocket had to arrange for extra chairs to be brought in from the church hall to accommodate the numbers. Florrie Bundy, the florist in Nutchester, had been ordered to deck out the church extravagantly and provide the bridal bouquet and buttonholes. Bob Wetherby, the local baker, had been ordered to bake a four-tier wedding cake par excellence. The Nutcombe Masonic Hall had been booked for the reception with Nonpareil Caterers providing a silver service. The principal guests were to be in morning suits and toppers and the bride would arrive at the church in a two-horse open carriage. If Mr and Mrs Fellowes had anything to do with it, it would be a perfect day. Indeed, in Mr Fellowes' inside pocket would reside a cheque to cover the happy couple's deposit on a house.

Emily received her invitation, artfully addressed to Mrs Grimshaw and kin-folk, and tempered her discomfiture with the knowledge that her financial position would improve with Stephen's departure.

Stephen himself bragged frequently to his mates about his conquest of such a lovely girl, while they, all Jack-the-lads, were amazed that this particular affaire had not been accompanied by accounts of his riotous bedroom antics, as all his previous liaisons had been. They ragged him ceaselessly about this strange aspect of his romance and demanded that he atone for his abstinence on his stag night. It had been arranged that they would go to the Kasbah night-club in Nutchester, have a few beers, and then search out the local talent.

At the same time that they were catching the bus into Nutchester, Grace sat at home making sure that all the details had been considered and settled, while in the local police station PC John Banks, aged twenty four, checked his notebook to remind himself of the details of the motoring offence about which he would be giving evidence in Nutchester Magistrates Court the following day.

The lads arrived at the Kasbah at eight o'clock to begin the serious business of getting plastered, and by nine o'clock they were half-way to their goal. Also in the Kasbah that night were supporters of the Cranbury Rugby Club which was to meet the Nutchester R.C. the following day. Now there are some topics which are taboo in certain circumstances. One must never tell a Frenchman that the French are poor lovers; or tell an American that the Yanks always enter wars towards the end; or tell an Aussie that they are lucky at cricket. But worse still, one must never tell Cranbury Rugby Club supporters, as Stephen and his mates did, that their team is as soft as cranberry sauce. The fight started in the bar, spread riotously across the dance-floor, up the stairs and into the street. In all there were a dozen or more participants, and blood was soon being splattered upon their shirts. The noise of battle alarmed the passers-by and nearby residents, and somebody phoned the police. Three police cars were quickly on the scene and the guardians of the law bravely stepped into the fray. With one eye closed and the other blurred by alcohol, Stephen lashed out randomly at whoever confronted him. It happened to be a police sergeant who received Stephen's right hook which sent the officer sprawling to the ground. Now there are some actions which are taboo in all circumstances, the main one being never to strike a policeman and hope to get away with it. Stephen didn't see the blow which floored him, and was only dimly aware that he was being handcuffed and on his way to the local nick.

He spent the night in a police cell bruised and bewildered, and only when he drank the mug of tea handed to him in the morning did the reality of his situation dawn upon him. He was locked up in Nutchester when he should be ten miles away in Nutcombe, preparing to be married at one o'clock.

At nine o'clock the custody sergeant came into his cell.

"Stephen Grimshaw, now that you are sober I am going to read you your rights. You do not have to say anything but anything you do say may be used in evidence. You are charged with assault upon a police officer causing actual bodily harm, affray, and being drunk and disorderly in a public place. You will be brought before the magistrate later this morning, round about eleven I should think. In the meantime you should tidy yourself up. You look as if you've been in a fight. Oh, sorry, of course you have been."

With that attempt at wit the sergeant left, leaving Stephen frantic with worry. If he was called at eleven there would be a mere two hours for his case to be heard, for him to get home to change and get to the church. He decided he would plead guilty to save time. He paced it out in his mind and reckoned that, with a bit of luck, he could just about fit it in.

Meanwhile in Nutcombe the villagers were preparing themselves for the grand occasion. Emily Grimshaw had splashed out on a new outfit, shoes and hat, for she wanted the world, or rather the men, to assume that she was much younger than she looked, and was still attractive in spite of having to care for her nephew for all those years. Mr Fellowes was busy at the Masonic Hall chivvying the caterers to ensure that the menu was exactly as he had ordered and that the place-cards were correctly located. Grace was seated in her bedroom having her hair arranged by Eugenie Lascelles, the proprietess of the local beauty salon, who was weaving it through the intricate head-dress forming part of the veil. Daisy Dimple was attending to Grace's manicure. Her fingernails were lacquered in the same attractive tone that had been applied to her toenails which now poked out from her satin peek-a-boo shoes. In the adjoining room the bridesmaids were helping each other into their dresses and preening themselves in front of the mirror. Downstairs Mrs Fellowes was frantically phoning Florrie Bundy to enquire about the bridal bouquet and the buttonholes, wiping away an occasional tear, but carefully so as not to smear her mascara. Inside the church the Rev. Cornelius Sprocket was bemoaning the fact that Mrs Eustacia Crabbe and Mrs Letitia Onions, his church workers, who were most energetic when it came to gossiping were less so when it came to helping him put out the extra chairs; and that the aged verger, Ephraim Binns, was bringing them in from the church hall one at a time. Elsewhere in Nutcombe the villagers were preparing themselves for the joyous occasion and putting on their Sunday best.

At eleven thirty Stephen stood in the dock facing the Stipendiary Magistrate, Mr Montague Middleton, a stern but fair man. His case took even less time than Stephen anticipated. He pleaded guilty to all the charges and the magistrate said, "Remanded in custody for seven days. Take him down."

"You can't do that, your honour!" cried Stephen. "I'm due to be married this afternoon! I can't be locked up!"

"You can and you will be," responded Mr Middleton. "You should have thought of your marriage instead of terrifying the neighbourhood last night."

"Please, your honour. I can't put my marriage off. If I don't get married today the chances are I won't ever marry my fiancée, Grace. You see, her parents aren't that keen on me marrying their daughter anyway, so if they knew I was in prison they'd talk her out of it."

It crossed the magistrate's mind that he would most probably be doing Grace a favour by locking him away.

"Look, your honour," continued Stephen, "I don't mind being remanded but I must get married first. You have no idea what a disappointment and expense it will be to all the people there. Scores of guests have been invited and will have travelled from far and wide, the caterers will have set out the tables, the church will be full of flowers, and all this will be wasted. All of us have hired our morning suits and what-have-you's, so it's not only me who will be punished but our families and guests. Please don't remand me for a week."

"You *will* be remanded, Mr Grimshaw. You have struck a police officer and that is a very serious offence."

"Your honour, I was drunk. I didn't intend to strike an officer. It was just a normal punch-up between blokes. Please think again. Let me at least get to the church to be married."

The magistrate was beginning to soften. Did it really matter, he pondered, if the prisoner was allowed freedom for a few hours? After all, that would not count as remand time to be taken off his eventual sentence. "Which church is that?" he finally asked.

"St Barnabas Parish Church in Nutcombe, your honour."

Mr Middleton shifted his gaze to the far end of the courtroom. "Usher!" he called. "See if that police officer who gave evidence in the motoring offence we heard earlier is still in the building." The usher left the courtroom and soon returned with PC John Banks.

"Constable," asked the magistrate, "are you returning to Nutcombe?"

"Yes, your honour."

"Well, I have a task for you. This prisoner has just been remanded in custody for a week but I am minded to order a stay of execution for this afternoon in order to allow him to be married at St Barnabas Parish Church. He has pleaded guilty to a very serious charge so I require him to be handcuffed to you throughout this afternoon, and when the ceremony has taken place and the reception is over he is to be brought back here. Is that clear?"

"Yes, your honour."

The magistrate addressed Stephen. "I can bend the rules no more than that, Mr Grimshaw. Go and get married and treat my leniency as a wedding present to you and your bride."

It was 12.15 p.m. when Stephen and Constable John Banks, handcuffed together, walked into the police car compound and approached the Nutcombe Police Wolseley.

"You'll have to get in from the driver's side and ease your way across to the passenger seat," said John.

"That's daft," retorted Stephen. "You won't be able to drive handcuffed to me. Take them off for while I'm in the car and put them back on again when we get out."

"You heard what the magistrate said, so now get in!"

"It's crazy! I'm sure he didn't mean it like you do."

"Shall we go back and ask him then?" John asked sarcastically. "You never know, he might be able to fit us in when he's heard all the other cases, but then of course we wouldn't get back to Nutcombe before all the guests have gone home. Now stop arguing and get in!"

Stephen accepted the inevitable and struggled across the front seats. John also had difficulty in getting himself into position, and gingerly drove out of the compound, forcing Stephen's right arm across, up and down every time he changed gear. In this fashion they made their way towards Nutcombe, with the minutes slowly ticking by.

"Can't you go any faster?" asked Stephen. "I've got to go home first to change."

"That would be hilarious!" scoffed John. "Just like a music-hall act. One bloke putting on a shirt and a jacket while handcuffed to another bloke."

"Jesus!" Stephen cried. "You're not even going to take them off then?"

"No, I'm not, and anyway, you don't have the time. We'll only just make it to the church as it is."

They arrived at St Barnabas Parish Church with five minutes to spare. They performed the difficult procedure of extricating themselves from the car and went inside. As they entered and began walking down the aisle a gasp went up from the guests. The assembled company had already been shaken by the number of Stephen's guests who bore visible signs of the previous night's punch up, but Stephen's appearance was in a different league altogether. He was unshaven and unkempt. One of his eyes was still closed, puffy and bruised. His cream-coloured pullover was splattered with blood and the collar of his shirt was torn partly away.

"He's a positive disgrace!" whispered the guest sitting next to Emily.

"I know, dear," she replied. "Whatever would his poor mother have said?"

John led his prisoner towards the front pew where sat the best man, sporting a split and swollen lip. John had to enter the row first, with Stephen occupying the seat by the aisle, visible for all to see. The Reverend Sprocket was shaken and approached Mrs Fellowes.

"I don't know what has happened, Mrs Fellowes, but should we continue?"

"We'd best wait until my husband arrives," she said. "He'd know best."

At that moment the usher standing at the church porch signaled to the organist that the bridal party had arrived, and the strains of Wagner's wedding march boomed throughout the church. Stephen and John joined the rest of the congregation in standing to see the bride approach. Grace, on her father's arm, looked astonishingly beautiful as she walked sedately down the aisle followed by the two bridesmaids holding her train. She reached the front of the church, raised her veil and looked lovingly towards her groom. Her gasp was heard by all present as Stephen moved to stand alongside her, closely followed by his police escort. She was totally bewildered at the sight facing her. Her groom was completely disheveled and handcuffed to a tall young policeman. She looked questioningly at John for an explanation and as their eyes met their lives changed for ever, for each in that instant knew that they were gazing at the love of their life. There was not the slightest doubt in either of their minds that they were instantly and deeply in love. They paid no attention to the vicar as he proceeded with the service, but gazed constantly at each other, communicating wordlessly, asking questions silently and receiving answers unspoken.

The vicar pressed on and began asking, "Do you, Stephen Arthur Grimshaw, take this woman, Grace Elizabeth Fellowes to be your lawful wedded wife", when John, still gazing intently at Grace, cried "*I* do! *I* do!" Grace felt her heart jump and she cried, "And I do to him, too!" Then, pushing Stephen aside, they spontaneously embraced each other and kissed, not once but several times, each kiss lasting longer and tasting sweeter. For a moment there was a stunned silence in the church until the romantic Daisy Dimple started to clap. The applause was taken up by other members of the congregation but not, needless to say, by Stephen's aunt Emily.

When it had died down, Mr Fellowes, business-like and pragmatic, stood up and addressed the guests. "It looks as if the wedding we planned is off, but I'm damned if I'm going to let the reception go to waste. So make your way to the Masonic Hall, forget what's happened and let's have a good time."

"All that expense for nothing," complained Mrs Fellowes.

"Look on the bright side, love. I'd prefer that young bobby to Grimshaw, any day, wouldn't you? Not only that, think of the money we've saved on the photographer!"

As the villagers slowly made their way out of the church and on to the Masonic Hall, Mr Fellowes approached John.

"Well, young man," he said, "Looks like you've made a conquest. Grace is coming with me and her mother to the reception and as it appears she's not going to let go of your arm it looks as if you'd better come too."

"I'd love to, sir," John replied, "but I've got to take Stephen back to Nutchester."

"Oh no!" Grace cried. "How long will you be gone?"

"I don't know. If I'm lucky I could be back in just over an hour."

"Oh, please be as quick as you can. I'll be waiting."

John said his goodbyes, kissed Grace yet again and drove away with a shell-shocked Stephen back to Nutchester. He had driven no more than a hundred yards when a thought struck him. The magistrate had ordered him to bring the prisoner back when the reception was over. Well, it hadn't even started! He took the next left hand turn and drove to the Nutcombe police station. He led Stephen inside and addressed the sergeant. "The magistrate has ordered me to bring this prisoner back to Nutchester later this evening, Sarge, so he should be locked in a cell until I come for him. And Sarge, don't stand any nonsense from him. He's pleaded guilty to assaulting a police sergeant last night so don't let him out of the cell."

"Oh, so he's the one, is he? I heard about that. Alright, sunshine, come along with me!"

With Stephen languishing in his cell, John made his way back to the Masonic Hall extremely happy with but one regret – that he would not be taking Grace on her planned honeymoon the next day – but he knew in his heart that that day would surely come.

* * *

THE WINNING TICKET

Albert Gold sat at home in his dressing gown and slippers listening with growing excitement to the Irish Sweepstake results being broadcast from Radio Luxembourg. As the programme reached its end he jumped up and cried, "I've won! I've won!" and promptly dropped down dead.

Mrs Gold sent for Dr Evans who duly pronounced that his death was the result of a heart attack, one that he long suspected would one day come. He said he would submit a death certificate in the morning and suggested that Mrs Gold might like to arrange for the undertaker to be notified.

Amos Lovejoy the undertaker duly arrived and assured Mrs Gold that Albert would be laid out respectfully and placed in the Chapel of Rest until all the funeral arrangements had been completed. He tactfully suggested that perhaps it would be more fitting if Albert were laid out in something other than pyjamas and dressing gown and so he was handed Albert's best suit and shoes, a clean shirt with a butterfly collar and a bow tie. This done, Albert was carried gently out of the house to the waiting hearse.

Two days later Amos Lovejoy called upon Mrs Gold to tell her that her dead husband was now nicely laid out and to give her a piece of screwed up paper on which was scrawled the names of a few horses and some numbers. "It was grasped in his hand so tightly," he explained, "that it took a while to get it free. Looks like Albert was planning to place a few bets at the races."

After the undertaker had left, Mrs Gold looked at the piece of paper in puzzlement. Albert had never been a serious betting man. In fact his only flutter was once a year on ……

"The Irish Sweepstake!" she exclaimed aloud, the truth striking her ferociously. "So that's what he meant when he said he had won! Cripes! That could be as much as £100,000! Now where could he have put that ticket?"

*

It was now the day before the funeral and Mrs Gold was a very worried woman. In the intervening period she had searched the house from top to bottom for the winning sweepstake ticket, again and again emptying drawers and cupboards in vain. That Albert had had such a ticket she was certain. She had seen it, and had even scolded him for his extravagance, but where he had he secreted it she was at a loss to know. After racking her brains for the umpteenth time, the awful truth dawned upon her. He must have placed it in one of the pockets of his best suit, the one he was now wearing as he lay at peace in his coffin!

There was not a moment to lose! She repaired at once to the funeral parlour with a story already firmly fixed in her mind, to keep her potential wealth a secret from all and sundry. She told Lovejoy that she wished to be left alone with Albert for a brief minute to say one last fond farewell and to cut off a lock of his hair as a touching memento.

"I'm sorry, Mrs Gold," Lovejoy said, "but the coffin lid has already been fastened down and there can be no question of opening it."

"But it wouldn't take long," she insisted. "It's only a matter of undoing a few screws."

"Only a few screws?" Lovejoy's voice rose. "Only a few screws? I'll have you know there's a full dozen and a half, solid brass, 2½ inch, countersunk and recessed, plugged with best pine dowelling, the ends of the plugs planed and sanded smooth, and finished with two coats of varnish. Only a few screws indeed!"

Eric, Lovejoy's assistant, opened his mouth to say something but closed it again sharply, but the gesture did not escape Mrs Gold's attention. She rightly guessed that Eric could see a possible solution to the problem but made one last attempt with Lovejoy.

"Please, Mr Lovejoy. I'll willingly pay for any additional expense, and possibly more."

"I'm sorry, Mrs Gold. The answer is 'no'. I'm closing up now. There's no more to be said." He put on his hat and coat, and addressed his assistant. "Sweep the workshop floor before you go, Eric, and be sure to lock up when you're done."

With Lovejoy gone, Mrs Gold turned to Eric. "OK, young man," she said. "You can see a solution. What is it?"

Eric leered. "First of all, what are you after, and what's in it for me?"

"What on earth are you saying?"

"Come on, you don't think I believe that nonsense about a fond farewell and a lock of hair, do you? We all know you and old Albert were at daggers drawn, so what's the game?"

Mrs Gold considered her position. This was the only opportunity she was ever going to have to search Albert's pockets before he was interred. If she did not seize it now it would be too late and any later attempt would require an exhumation which would undoubtedly raise a few eyebrows. She decided to come clean – well, almost.

"You're right. I need to search my departed husband's pockets. He always carried a £20 note in his suit to cover any emergencies, and I clean forgot about it when I handed the suit to Lovejoy. So if you let me retrieve it I will give you £5."

Eric laughed. "£5? You're joking. If it's £20 then I'll need half!"

"That's ridiculous! The £5 I'm offering is more than you earn in a week."

"Half!" insisted Eric. "Take it or leave it!"

Mrs Gold conceded. What was £10 against the £100,000 she would be gaining. "OK, agreed. So what's the plan? Take the bottom off the coffin then?"

Eric looked at her with contempt. "The base is dovetail jointed. We make coffins, Mrs Gold, not orange boxes. No, we'll cut a hole in the bottom, and then patch it up when we've got the bank note. Nobody ever sees the bottom of a coffin, do they? Here, help me turn the coffin over."

Together they managed to turn the coffin onto its top. The thud as Albert's corpse shifted position was momentarily unnerving, but once it had settled face downward all was still again. Eric set to work with a briskness which would have surprised Lovejoy to see. With a brace and bit he bored four holes in the bottom, marking the corners of a square. In the centre of the square he made a small hole with a gimlet and screwed a large cup-hook into it. Then he took a pad saw and sawed out the sides of the square. Using the cup-hook as a handle he removed the detached piece, leaving a hole about a foot square.

Mrs Gold pushed him aside and thrust her hand into the opening and rummaged around.

"Don't be daft," said Eric. "There's the lining to be got through first. Here, I'll do it." He had already taken his prized Swiss Army penknife from his pocket and opened its largest blade, with which he now rent a long slit in the satin-effect lining of the coffin. He inserted his arm and tried to feel for the note, but soon gave up. "It's no good; he's too tight a fit.

There's no room to get round him. We'll just have to cut the jacket off him," said Eric, secretly enjoying the opportunity for ruthless destruction. Ripping through the stitching with his knife, he opened the back seam of Albert's jacket from hem to collar. Albert still had his arms through the garment, so Eric reached up and cut through both of the shoulder seams. As the last stitch gave way, he uttered an oath.

"What's up?" asked Mrs Gold. "Have you cut yourself?"

"No, I've dropped my penknife."

"Never mind that, I'll buy you a new one. Just get the jacket."

Eric took hold of one side of the garment and pulled firmly, but it would not budge. "He's too heavy," he declared. "We'll have to tilt the coffin to get his weight off it."

They slid the foot of the coffin over the end of the table, Eric working one-handed as he retained a grip on the jacket through the hole. The coffin teetered a moment when its centre of gravity reached the table's edge, then suddenly fell to the floor. It almost escaped their grasp as Albert's weight slid down, but their combined exertions steadied it in an upright position leaning against the table. Eric extracted his arm and triumphantly flourished the jacket, still buttoned down the front.

"Good lad! Give us it here," urged Mrs Gold.

"As soon as we've got this back on the table," agreed Eric.

They shifted their grip to the foot of the coffin and heaved until they had lifted it horizontal again and could slide it onto the table. Once they could let go, Eric passed the jacket to Mrs Gold and set about repairing the coffin.

From under the bench he took a few offcuts of 2"x1" softwood battens, each about eighteen inches long, and slid these inside, one on top of the other, filling the gap between

Albert's back and the inner surface of the base. He then replaced the sawn-out piece of the bottom. It was only a loose fit, owing to the thickness of the saw cuts, but the battens supported it at its original level. He mixed a handful of sawdust with glue, and forced it down into the gap around the edges with a putty knife. This masterpiece of bodgery he completed by applying a layer of glue across and beyond the patch, and affixing a sheet of brown paper. He stepped back and surveyed his handiwork with satisfaction.

Mrs Gold was also pleased with the outcome, and quietly slipped the winning Irish Sweepstake ticket into her purse.

"Right," said Eric, "just help me turn the coffin over."

They turned the coffin the right way up again, this time without any disconcerting movement from within, Albert now being wedged up against the lid by Eric's battens. Once Mrs Gold had left, after promising to see him right the next day, Eric locked up and went home.

*

On the following day the funeral service at the church went without a hitch. Mrs Gold's grief attracted much sympathy, Eric being the only one who knew it was contrived. The cortège moved to the cemetery, where six stalwart pall bearers began to carry the coffin to the waiting grave. Smooth though their progress was, the slight jolting was enough to cause a movement of the battens on which Albert was resting. A piece slipped out of place, and the corpse fell an inch or two.

The pall bearers felt the movement. One or two stopped in their tracks, bringing them all to a stumbling halt. Vainly they tried to catch each other's eyes, every man loath to be the first to voice the awful thought they all shared. The vicar, the aged

Rev. Cornelius Sprocket, who was leading the procession with his nose in the Book of Common Prayer, sensed that he was no longer being followed, and turned back with some annoyance at this threat to the solemnity of the occasion.

"Come, come, what seems to be the problem?"

"He moved," said the boldest of the pall bearers.

"He's still alive," added another.

Albert's weight was now pressing the end of a batten into the middle of Eric's makeshift repair. Unable to sustain the pressure, it gave way with an audible crack. A piece of wood fell to the path, and a fold of tattered lining spilled out of the coffin.

"'E's trying to get out!" shrilled young Billy Enright.

All decorum was gone. Of those following the coffin, some tried to distance themselves in fear, while others pressed closer in curiosity.

"This really won't do," was the vicar's less than helpful contribution.

"You can't bury someone who's still alive," said one bystander, looking accusingly at the vicar and Lovejoy in turn.

"Phone for an ambulance," suggested another.

Mrs Gold, who at the church had done her best to look stricken by Albert's death, was now rather more successfully looking distraught at the prospect of his still being alive. Aware that his reputation as the organizer of high-class funerals was evaporating by the minute, Lovejoy took command. He had the pall bearers retrace their steps and return the coffin to the hearse. While they were doing so an ambulance arrived, summoned by the cemetery caretaker. Lovejoy explained the situation to the driver, and citizens lucky enough to be abroad that Sunday were entertained by the sight of an ambulance driving at high speed, lights flashing, bell ringing, from the cemetery to the funeral parlour, followed by a hearse proceeding at the same breakneck pace.

In his workshop Lovejoy frantically attacked the coffin lid, boring out the dowels and removing the screws with his biggest Stanley pump-action ratchet screwdriver, watched by a small group of onlookers who had followed the coffin from the cemetery in order, as one put it, "not to be in at the kill so much as to be in at the resurrection." When the lid came off, there were gasps of horror at the disorder revealed.

"Poor man. He must have been in agony."

"You can see how much he struggled to get out."

Lovejoy spotted the pen knife, the blade still open, and removed it. This excited further comment. "He even tried to cut his way out."

The doctor who had signed Albert's death certificate arrived, alerted by the ambulance station. He elbowed his way to the front and took in the scene.

"I can't examine a man in a coffin. Get him out."

Albert was removed and laid out on the table. The doctor examined him thoroughly before announcing, with some acidity, "This man is dead. He was dead when I examined him five days ago. He is dead now. It is my professional opinion that he has been dead every instant of the interim."

A voice from the back was heard to mutter a remark that included the words "second opinion."

The doctor turned to the ambulance crew and made a gesture that indicated "He's all yours."

The ambulance men took it in turns to examine Albert, and delivered their verdict. "He's dead all right."

The ambulance driver asked his colleagues "What do we do now, then? Take him to the casualty department?"

The doctor demurred, foreseeing that if a second death certificate were issued for the same corpse, complications might ensue. "If I were you, I'd leave him here, and mark the call down as a malicious hoax," he suggested.

"Who called us, then?" asked the driver, looking around. Nobody volunteered to take the credit.

After a short consultation the ambulance men marked their job sheet "Well intentioned false alarm" and left, followed by the doctor. Casual sightseers began to drift away, sensing that the show was over.

Lovejoy detained the pall bearers and Eric. He was now lumbered with a corpse at a time when he should have been at home calculating his profit, but, damaged though it was, the coffin was still serviceable, and an empty grave still awaited at the cemetery. If he hurried, there might yet be time to complete the day's undertaking. He had already noticed the opening in the bottom of the coffin, and had put a piece of plywood over it.

"Here, help me get him back in his box."

When Albert's corpse had been unceremoniously returned to the coffin, Lovejoy replaced the lid and fastened it with just four screws. "Well," he thought to himself, "that really makes twenty-two altogether." To Eric he said, "Help me get this casket on to the hearse. Let's hope the vicar and the mourners are still there. And don't think that that's the end of it! I'll see you tomorrow and give you back your penknife - and your cards."

The hearse arrived at the cemetery just in time to stop the vicar from calling it a day. The burial concluded as originally planned, though the onlookers all agreed that it was more exciting the first time around.

*

The following morning Lovejoy confronted Eric. "I suppose you realize that you have ruined me?" he asked. "Who will give me their business when news of that fiasco gets around? They will all be going to other firms now."

Eric was neither intelligent nor educated, but he possessed a natural cunning which served him well. "They might go to another firm first, Mr Lovejoy, but they will come back here if the other firm won't give them what they want and you will."

"What they want? What do you mean?"

"I've been listening to people talk, Mr Lovejoy. They are all afraid of being buried alive. They are saying that there should be some way of getting out of a coffin without having to cut your way out with a penknife."

"I still don't see what you're driving at."

"You can be the first, Mr Lovejoy - be the first to offer a coffin with a quick-release mechanism inside. You'll corner the market, guvnor, I'm sure you will."

"That's all very well, but where am I to get this special quick-release mechanism you talk of? If such a thing existed I'm sure it would have been advertised in the Undertakers Journal."

"It doesn't have to be special, Mr Lovejoy. An ordinary door latch will do."

And so the Lovejoy Peace-of-Mind® casket was born. It resembled a normal coffin, but the lid was fastened with hinges on one side and a door latch on the other, rather like a cupboard but with the vital difference that the doorknob was on the inside.

"The beauty of it is," said Lovejoy to his wife, claiming the invention as his own, "that it is quicker and cheaper to make, but people are willing to pay more for it."

The deluxe version had discreet air vents around the top of the sides, and a clockwork doorbell for summoning aid. Eric had suggested clips for holding a packet of sandwiches and a flask of tea, but Lovejoy thought that such luxury would need a higher class of clientele than he was likely to command.

Eric's predictions proved to be correct. Mourners who enquired at the Co-operative Funeral Parlour for a coffin permitting easy exit were mocked and escorted from the premises, while other customers suffered similar indignities elsewhere. At Lovejoy's, however, they were received with sympathy and understanding, and it was widely acknowledged that he was, after all, the only undertaker in the district with experience in the matter of premature burial. In time the details of Albert's funeral were forgotten, and Lovejoy's trade returned to normal. Older inhabitants, however, still refer to the occasion as The Day That Albert Gold Was Buried Alive.

* * *

JOYCE THE VERGER

As long-serving members of the congregation of the Parish Church of St Barnabas, Mrs Eustacia Crabbe and Mrs Letitia Onions, saw their comfortable past being shattered before their very eyes. For decades they had become used to the same male and malleable triumvirate of vicar, verger and church warden who, despite their spiritual authority in the village, were subject to their domination. But then two events had upset the even tenor of their ways.

First, the vicar, the Rev. Cornelius Sprocket, had died of a heart attack whilst judging the Village Beauty Queen contest at the May Festival, (won by Daisy Dimple, 36,28,34), to be replaced by the Rev. Claud Higgins, who was far less than half the age of the over-excitable Sprocket.

Secondly, the services of Ephraim Binns the verger had been dispensed with after he had been found singing lewd songs in the crypt, surrounded by empty communion wine bottles. His replacement was, according to Eustacia and Letitia, a mere chit of a girl.

Only the church warden, Wilkinson Grudbear, had stood firm before the oncoming tide of progress, but since he was now in his late eighties the ladies knew in their hearts that he too would soon be swamped. Nevertheless they were determined to make the lives of the newcomers as difficult as possible.

*

The new verger was Joyce McNaughtie, a charming girl in her mid-twenties, extremely attractive and stylishly dressed. She came from a well-to-do family which allowed her to buy her clothes, always in the latest fashion, from LadyChic of Bond Street in London. To satisfy her personal indulgence the store embroidered her initials, JMcN, on all her undergarments, scarves and gloves. Joyce was a dedicated Christian, who was most conscientious about her lay duties, but many in the congregation found it difficult to take her seriously, so different was she from her predecessor. When parishioners saw her walking gaily along the street, dressed in the height of fashion, they found it difficult to reconcile her with the studious verger dressed solemnly in her black cassock with fascia and jabot, carrying out her duties at the various church services.

Joyce sensed the residual resentment but was determined not to let it upset her. She carried out her duties joyfully and with a lightness of spirit which had more than a little to do with the feelings she had towards the vicar. The Rev. Claud Higgins was just turned thirty, diffident but good-natured. Joyce's feelings towards him had grown throughout her first year and she took whatever opportunity she could to help him and be close. They were often to be seen together, laughing easily and intimately as only very good friends can. Claud was unaware that he was being wooed and would have been astonished to read Joyce's mind as she sat listening to his serious sermons, but Fate was about to bring matters to a head that evening.

Joyce had finished washing her smalls, a practice she carried out most evenings. She rinsed them along with other items and took them into the garden to hang upon the line. This done, she went back indoors and got ready for bed. During the night a wind got up, strong enough to bend over shrubs and send dustbin lids flying. It tugged away at Joyce's washing, finally snatching her smalls from off the line. It carried them along the lane and over rooftops until they reached the churchyard where, in the lee of the yew trees, they settled upon the vicarage lawn. It was there that they were found the following morning by the two self-appointed vigilantes, Mrs Crabbe and Mrs Onions. Realising that bras and panties are not usually to be found on vicarage lawns they picked them up and scrutinised them. They were struck immediately by the fineness of the material, the workmanship and the delicate embroidery, then, spotting Joyce's embroidered initials, they were aghast.

"Brazen hussy!" shrieked Mrs Crabbe, holding the bra aloft. "This is a 36D! No self-respecting woman wears a 36D!" There was a real touch of anguish behind her jealousy, as she herself wore no bra at all, her husband's man-boobs being much larger than her own rudimentary paps. "And what are they doing on the vicarage lawn? What was she up to that she had to take them off?"

"And she had to go home without them, too," volunteered Mrs Onions, a 42 double E if ever there was one. "You're right, Eustacia. She's a brazen hussy!"

"But what about the vicar in all of this, Letitia?" demanded Mrs Crabbe with a knowing air. "If she was dancing naked in front of the vicarage, he must have been involved too, mustn't he?"

They looked at each other with glowing eyes, knowing that they had in their hands the means of bringing down both vicar and verger, but only if they handled the matter correctly. "Let's keep this to ourselves for the time being, Letitia," said Mrs Crabbe, stuffing the undies into her handbag, "until I've thought about it a bit more."

Having thought about it all day, she set in motion her whispering campaign. She whispered the details, suitably embellished, to the Women's Temperance Society, to the Bridge Circle and to Mrs Pollifax with her psychic circus. Any woman who expressed doubts was shown the monogrammed bra and panties, which clearly could never have been worn by Mrs Crabbe, and so became convinced. In time, as all the recipients of the scandalous news added their own refinements to the story which was widely discussed in hushed tones throughout the gossiping classes, Mrs Crabbe decided that she now had the incontrovertible proof she needed to take the matter to the church authorities, namely the church warden, Wilkinson Grudbear.

She headed the delegation which marched along the church path, into the church, along the aisle then left at the altar into the vestry where they knew the church warden would be after his visit to the Red Lion, asleep in the vicar's chair. They shook him awake and regaled him with their dramatic news. His rheumy eyes opened wide as they recounted the satanic happenings, and as their stories unfolded he needed little convincing that it was his duty to report to the Bishop the ghastly happenings centring upon the vicar and his familiar, the verger. For the rest of the day he penned his missive, aided and abetted by a smugly smiling Mrs Crabbe.

*

The Bishop of Nutchester, the Rt. Rev. Dr Robert Swineforth, was attended by his secretary, the Rev. Desmond Bland, as they discussed his many appointments and future itinerary, for the Bishop was to accompany the Archbishop on his visit to the Anglican Bishops in Africa, which included a three-week tour of their dioceses. "I think that buttons everything up, don't you, Desmond?" asked the Bishop at last.

"Well, there is just one matter, my lord, that I think needs your immediate attention, and that is a disturbing letter you have just received from the church warden at Nutcombe."

"Who is he?"

"Mr Wilkinson Grudbear."

"Old Wilkie?" the Bishop cried. "I thought he would have snuffed it ages ago. He must be nearly a hundred."

"Eighty-seven, my lord," corrected his secretary.

"Well, what's he got to say?"

"I think you had better read it, my lord," responded the Rev. Desmond, as he handed over the letter. The Bishop adjusted his glasses and began to read, then said, "I can't read a thing! It looks as if some spider with ink on its feet has crawled over the pages. You'll have to read it to me."

The secretary took back the letter, cleared his throat and read aloud:

"Right Reverend Sir,

It pains me greavously to have to inform you of the satanic hapnings which started to occur upon the pointment of our new vicar and his verger and which now has reached dramatick preportions. I have it on the authoraty of ladies of unpeachible, not to say unpeckable cridentials that the following hapnings have been witnessed, namely and to wit.

One: on April 30th last, Wally Perkins nite, lites were seen in the woods and upon investigation by the ladies they saw sevral naked girls dancing round a fire chanting rude songs.

Two: Sexual orgies can be heard taking place near the cricket pavilion most evenings, though of course the ladies do not stay to witniss such deborchary.

Three: Pagan rites take place at the village hall evry Thursday.

Four: Witch's caverns exist but are suspishusly secret so we don't know who or where.

Five and most important: Three nites ago the verger was seen dancing naked in front of the vicar without shame, bra or nickers, displaying her unbridled lust and stremely well developed bust. I have seen the evidents which prove this.

For these reasons, Right Reverend Sir, we think you should order an indipandant and impartial inquiry and sack the pair of them.

I remain,
Your obediant servant,
Wilkinson Grudbear (church warden)."

"What utter nonsense!" cried the Bishop. "Wally Perkins Night indeed! Chuck it in the wagga pagga!"

"You may well be right, my lord," said Desmond, "but it would surely be better to deal with it as if it were serious. After all, if there is something in it, we wouldn't wish to be shown to be dismissive without due enquiry."

"You're right as always, Desmond. Send it to the Diocesan Registrar for Preliminary Scrutiny with a covering note. Then send a letter to old Wilkie saying I have started the necessary proceedings and will keep him informed. Oh, and send a letter to the vicar, that's young Higgins, isn't it? Tell him we have received a serious complaint about him and his parish which is receiving our urgent attention." With that the Bishop left his palace, not to return until three weeks had elapsed.

*

Both letters duly arrived in Nutcombe to markedly different reactions by the recipients.

The church warden, Mrs Crabbe and her cronies were delighted and saw the outcome as inevitable. The Bishop was taking the matter seriously which clearly showed that he was on their side. It was thus only a matter of time before vicar and verger were sacked. No longer needing to be courteous or respectful towards either of them, they displayed hostility and unhelpfulness towards both.

On receiving his letter, Claud was astonished. Who could possibly be complaining and about what? He asked the church warden if he could throw any light on it, but Wilkinson Grudbear sneered and walked on without answering. Claud found himself snubbed.

He sought advice from Joyce, who herself had begun to notice the changed atmosphere surrounding her work, but she was equally mystified, and found herself ostracised by the vinegary element of the congregation.

As day followed day they felt the hostility growing, and as day followed day the poisonous rumours did their work. Joyce felt particularly vulnerable. She was by nature exceptionally friendly, which normally brought with it a corresponding response. But not anymore. For over a week she had been ostracised by most of the church workers and had begun to question her vocation.

One morning she entered Henry Lambton's butcher's shop to collect her order and found him trying to placate the tall and gorgeous Kitty Dowd who was complaining about the size of the meat ration.

"One shilling and tuppence worth of meat a week!" cried Kitty. "How am I supposed to cater for my Daniel's most enormous appetite with such a paltry portion?"

On seeing Joyce enter the shop the butcher greeted her cheerfully, glad of the opportunity to change the subject.

"Hello, Joyce," he said. "I was thinking about you earlier today when old Billy Watkins and I were having our usual theosophical discussion. I made the point to him that if there was a God, he must have a sense of humour. By way of explanation I said that the sweetest meat of all was oxtail, but that God had designed the animal so that its tail was located just above its dirtiest part, the bum hole. Now if that doesn't reveal a sense of humour I don't know what does. Billy laughed at that and said that that was a nice point to put to the vicar or the verger. So what do you think, Joyce? Has God got a sense of humour?"

"Well," sighed Joyce, "if He has designed the present atmosphere throughout the parish I don't find it the slightest bit funny. God alone knows what it's all about."

Kitty sensed Joyce's sorrow, and as they left the shop she laid her hand gently on Joyce's arm. "You obviously don't know the rumours, Joyce. Some people are saying that you and the vicar are lovers."

"What! I can't believe it! How could you say such a thing?" cried Joyce.

"It's not me. I'm just letting you know what people are saying. You aren't, though, are you?"

"Certainly not! Not that I'd mind if we were. Unfortunately as far as Claud is concerned I'm more Joyce the virgin than Joyce the verger."

Kitty stopped walking and took her arm again. She looked her in the face and asked in a serious tone, "Do you really mean what you said about not minding if you were lovers?"

"Yes," replied Joyce, "I meant every word, but he's so bloody shy. I drop all sorts of hints and suggestions and he just gets sheepish."

Kitty laughed aloud. "You goose!" she said. "People are cutting you dead because they think you are sleeping with the vicar, and though you are upset by this, you nonetheless wish that what they are saying was true. So do yourself a favour! If you're being forced to do the time, you should at least enjoy the crime!"

"You mean..." began Joyce.

"Yes!" cried Kitty. "But don't just drop hints and suggestions. Show him!"

Joyce smiled her thanks to Kitty then rushed away back home. After she had showered, and dabbed herself with her favourite perfume, she put on her most revealing bra and her daintiest panties, dressed herself in her most stylish outfit, and walked purposefully into the vicarage. In a little over ten minutes, the rumours about her and Claud being lovers became true, and they were able to enjoy their conjugal bliss for many days.

This development frustrated Mrs Crabbe, for the whole point of her malicious rumour was to hurt the victims – but if the victims did not mind the hurt, what was the point?

"They're masochists!" she hissed.

*

The Bishop returned from his African visit and entered once again into his diocesan workload. "What about that Nutcombe nonsense?" he asked his secretary.

"The Diocesan Registrar agrees. It is nonsense and asks whether it isn't time for Grudbear to be asked to retire."

"Good!" said the Bishop. "So that's the end of that."

"Not quite, my lord," said Desmond. "We have had a further letter that the vicar and the verger are now cohabiting in the vicarage. This is true, as I have been able to confirm for myself."

"Dear Lord!" sighed the Bishop. "Whatever have I done to deserve that parish? Fix a day for me to visit Nutcombe unannounced."

In due course that day arrived. It was a Thursday and the church calendar was clear. Claud was lounging in the sitting room of the vicarage, with the gramophone playing records of Leslie Hutchinson. Joyce was upstairs trying on a new set of undies which had just arrived from LadyChic of Bond Street, when the door bell sounded. Claud turned down the volume and opened the front door.

"Jesus!" he gasped in astonishment.

"No, just the Bishop," said the Rt..Rev. Dr Robert Swineforth striding into the room. "I take it you're Claud Higgins. Turn off that awful music, sit down and answer a few questions. First, have you somebody living here with you?"

"Yes, my Lord."

"Who?"

Claud sagged visibly. "It's the verger, my Lord," he replied.

"For Heaven's sake!" cried the Bishop. "Why the devil couldn't you have said the housekeeper? That's what we used to say in my young day! But the verger! Have you no sense? I always knew it was wrong to allow women vergers. I wouldn't be surprised if they even campaigned for women priests next!"

At that moment Joyce appeared in order to get Claud's opinion on her new negligee, and very sexy she looked in it, too. She skipped merrily into the living room, pirouetting on one foot, twirled around, flung out her arms and cried "Ta-da!" stopping face to face with the astonished Bishop. It would be difficult to say who was the more surprised.

"Joyce!" the Bishop cried.

"Gosh! Er - Hello, Uncle!" she responded.

"What the dickens are you doing here? I thought you were doing voluntary service overseas."

"I decided to stay in England, Uncle, and took up this post."

The Bishop took off his glasses and wiped them with his handkerchief slowly and thoroughly to give himself time to think. "You two have put me in a terrible mess, you know. This is getting to be like some French farce. I have got to respond to the letter I have received, and having personally seen the truth in it, I can only see one way out, and that is for the pair of you to get married. And you *will* marry her, my boy, if you know what's good for your career. Now I must be off. It wouldn't do for me to be seen condoning your affair."

With that he left, leaving Claud and Joyce with questions of their own. "Why have you never told me you were the Bishop's niece?" Claud asked.

"Why?" she laughed. "You are so bloody shy I would never have got you into bed with me if you had known that. Anyway, that wasn't what I thought you were going to ask me."

"What was that?"

"Well, aren't you going to ask me to marry you?"

"Yes, of course. I suppose I have no other choice now that the Bishop has threatened me if I don't."

"You are silly!" Joyce said. "I know my uncle better than you do. What he meant was that being the Bishop's nephew-in-law would benefit your career no end!"

* * *

THE BIGAMIST

Peter Penny was the village blacksmith, a gentle giant of a man, known and respected by the villagers for miles around. His forge was situated behind the garage and petrol station on the approach to Nutcombe, and a thriving business he had too, for in addition to his farrier work he had built up a large clientele for his decorative wrought-iron work. It was mid-morning when he saw the local bobby approaching on his bike. He laid his hammer and tongs on the workbench, wiped his hands on his leather apron and held out his hand to greet his visitor, PC John Banks.

"How are you, John," he said, "and your lovely Grace? I haven't seen much of you since the wedding."

"We're very well, Peter, and thank you for asking, but...."

"And the baby? How's he, or she, coming along?"

"Everything's fine, Peter, but ..."

"I don't think I'll ever forget that day in church. Have you seen anything of Stephen Grimshaw since?"

"I heard he got married to a girl Nutchester way."

"Well it didn't take long to mend his broken heart then," laughed Peter, "especially with his Aunt Emily bringing pressure to bear!"

The policeman stirred uneasily. "Peter," he said, "this is not a social call. I've got some very bad news for you. Information has been laid that you have five wives."

"Yes, I know I have, John. It's no secret. Everybody knows it, including you, so what's the fuss all about?"

Indeed, all the villagers knew that, in addition to Peggy, his wife in Nutcombe, the blacksmith had wives in four of the surrounding villages. Jane was the Brankton wife; Elsie the one in Gifford; Iris in Little Parsley and Milly in Felsham. It was a common sight to see Peter mount his bicycle when he had finished his day's work at the forge and cycle off towards the crossroads. Onlookers would see which way he turned and say, "It's Elsie's turn this evening." or "Oh, he's going to Milly's to read his little 'un a bedtime story." It was commonplace and taken for granted. Villagers no longer paid any attention to it.

"Peter, it's serious," insisted the policeman. "Somebody has laid this information and I have got to follow it up."

"But who would report it? What could they possibly get out of it?"

"Someone with a grudge, perhaps?"

"Why should anyone bear a grudge towards me?" Peter asked. "I've never hurt anyone."

"The information was laid by someone in Little Parsley, that's all I know."

Peter furrowed his brow a while and then grunted. "Brenda Wilson! That's the one! She said I would regret it."

"Regret what?"

"She asked me if she could be my next wife, and I had to turn her down. She obviously took it harder than I thought."

"You turned down Brenda Wilson? I can think of a lot of lads who wouldn't say no to that offer. Don't you fancy her, then?"

"It's not that," Peter explained. "She lives in Little Parsley and I've already got a wife there. I make it a rule to keep my wives apart. If I had two in the same village and went to visit one, the other would complain, 'Why are you visiting her instead of me?' Or the two of them would meet in the street and be bitchy towards each other. As it is, because my wives are in separate villages they see each other only rarely, on market days and the like, and treat each other as sisters, because that's what they are, sisters-in-law. Perhaps I should have explained that to Brenda," he added ruefully.

"Well, whoever it was, the complaint's been laid and I'm afraid I've got to arrest you. I'm sorry, Peter, but you've got to come with me to the station."

"What, now? I can't do that, John. You know that. I've work to do. The squire wants his hunter re-shod this afternoon. I'll pop along after I've finished work."

"Peter, if it were left to me I'd say OK, but if I don't bring you in, the sergeant will charge me with disobedience or something."

The blacksmith laughed. "The sergeant, eh? You tell him I'll be along later, and if he gets stroppy tell him I mentioned something about a wrought-iron lantern."

"A wrought-iron lantern? What's that got to do with anything?"

"Just tell him that. He'll understand, and there'll be no bother."

*

The blacksmith was summoned to appear before the Magistrates Court in Nutchester two weeks later and released on police bail. He was a worried man after Ron Baker, the licensee of the Red Lion, had told him that, unfair though it was, he could end up in jail.

"That's ridiculous! Who'd look after my wives and kiddies if I'm locked up? And why now? I've had my wives for years without any fuss or bother."

"It's the law, Peter," explained Ron.

"Well, the law's an ass in that case. But I reckon the police have got it wrong. They're reading the law wrongly. I reckon it all needs looking into."

So Peter caught the bus to Nutchester and spent half a day in the Reference Library studying Law. Satisfied that he had found the police's regrettable misreading of the Law, he returned to Nutcombe in a happy frame of mind, eagerly awaiting his coming encounter in court.

The day of the arraignment arrived and the villages buzzed with excitement. The blacksmith had hired a char-a-banc for the occasion, festooned with banners demanding justice for multi-wived husbands. The procession started from the Nutcombe village war memorial, with Peter and PC Banks positioned in the front seats and Peggy and her five-year-old son behind. The villagers cheered and waved as the char-a-banc set off to make its way around the countryside, picking up the other wives and offspring from their respective villages. Throughout its progress through the highways and byways villagers and onlookers clapped and waved until it finally reached the Magistrates Court and the occupants disembarked and trooped into the courtroom.

When Peter's case was called he went into the dock. "Peter Penny," the Clerk intoned, "you have been charged with four counts of bigamy. How do you plead?"

"Not guilty!" he proclaimed loudly.

Mr Middleton, the magistrate leaned towards him. "Mr Penny, I understand that your wives are here in this courtroom. Is that correct?"

"Yes, your honour."

"And yet you are pleading 'not guilty'?"

"That's right, your honour."

"But surely their presence here does not support your 'not guilty' plea?"

"They're here to give evidence in mitigation, your honour."

"Mitigation? But you've pleaded not guilty!"

"In the alternative, your honour. In the alternative."

How speedily the layman learns the lawyers' lingo, and after just one afternoon in the Library!

"Very well," said the magistrate. "Proceed."

As the wives were called to the stand they acknowledged that yes, they did marry the blacksmith on such and such a date, and yes, they did know that Peter had other wives, but they pointed out that this was their affair, and no-one else's.

Elsie said that if Peter were sent to jail their young son's education would be disrupted, for Peter was teaching him about metals, their composition and their use, so that the lad could achieve his ambition to become a metallurgist.

Iris said that she was not in perfect health, so if she had a recurrence and Peter was in jail, he would not be able to nurse her for a whole week as once he had done.

Milly said that she and the other wives had spent hours embroidering a wedding gown for Peter's next bride. They were to be maids of honour at the forthcoming wedding. Was all their needlework to be in vain? Mr Middleton nearly choked as he sipped his water.

Jane said that she demanded the restoration of convivial nights. The clerk whispered to the magistrate, "I believe the witness means the restitution of conjugal rights."

"I know what I flipping well meant!" cried Jane.

When Peter was about to give his evidence from the dock, the magistrate leant forward across the Bench and said, "Penny, I must warn you that I will take a very serious view if I find that you are deliberately wasting the court's time with a frivolous defence. On all the evidence I have heard so far, and upon your own admission, you now have five wives. How can you possibly plead not guilty?"

Peter pulled his shoulders back, grasped the lapels of his jacket and adopted the pose of seasoned Q.C. "Oh, I admit the *actus reus*, your honour, but not the *mens rea*. I admit the guilty act, but not the guilty mind."

"I know what the terms mean, Mr Penny," the magistrate retorted testily, "but I do not see how that helps you."

"Well, your honour, as I understand it, a person cannot be guilty of an offence if at the time it can be shown that it was not his intention to commit that offence. The presumption of *mens rea* is an essential ingredient in all cases, and in my present case I state on oath that it was not my intention to commit bigamy."

Mr Middleton shook his head in disbelief. "But you married these four women knowing that you were already legally married! How can you possibly argue that it was not your intention to commit bigamy?"

"I did not go to the church with the *intention* of committing bigamy. My sole *intention* was to marry them, because I love them. I admit that bigamy was a necessary consequence, but that consequence was not of my doing and was certainly not my intention. Look, your honour, it's like this. I go to the swimming baths to have a swim. I dive in and get wet. If someone asks me 'did you dive in to get wet?' I would say 'No. My intention was to swim, but a necessary concomitant to that was getting wet.'"

"And the Law, Mr Penny, says that the concomitant to marrying a woman when you are already legally married is the chargeable offence of bigamy."

"I know," responded the now well-versed blacksmith. "But that same Law protects a person without *mens rea*, which must be presumed in all cases."

Mr Middleton changed tack. "You made certain promises at your wedding ceremonies, did you not, Mr Penny."

"Yes sir, I did, and I've kept every one. I love and honour all my wives."

"What about the promise to forsake all others?"

"I was absolved of those promises, your honour, every time. Before I marry an additional wife I ask my existing wives for their consent, and that I have done in every case."

"That's right, your honour," cried the wives.

"But you were married in church, were you not, so you also made those promises to God."

"True, but with respect, your honour, I think that's for Him to judge, don't you?"

Mr Middleton leant forward and conversed briefly with the clerk of the court who announced, "The court will recess for ten minutes. Please remain seated."

Mr Middleton and the clerk left the chamber taking with them two massive tomes. Upon the magistrate's return he addressed the blacksmith directly. "Mr Penny, I have had a chance to research your ingenious defence, and now regret to tell you that it has failed. As you rightly pointed out, *mens rea* is an essential ingredient of every offence and must be presumed in all cases, unless – and this is a crucial point - unless statute provides otherwise, and where statute does so provide, the liability is strict. I now have to tell you that statute provides that bigamy is one such crime. On your own admission that you have four wives in addition to your legally married wife there can be no doubt whatsoever that the law requires a 'guilty' verdict.

"Having said that, I am minded to say that I have been singularly impressed by your demeanour towards those women and by their glowing testimony of you. I am forced to admit that were you but a philandering scallywag, seducing women around the countryside, neglecting them and their children and leaving them destitute, I would have absolutely no power to bring any sanction against you. But even though you are not a scallywag, but a responsible member of society, loving and caring for your families, I am obliged to find you guilty. This I do with a heavy heart, but I have no choice. Mr Penny, the verdict of this Court is that you are guilty ..." (there was a gasp throughout the courtroom), "... and I hereby sentence you to six months imprisonment, suspended for 12 months. I must warn you, Mr Penny, if you marry another woman during that period you will be brought before this Court and severely punished." He smiled, then added, "Now you are free to leave at your many wives' pleasure."

* * *

[Editor's note: Older readers may recall that the blacksmith's case reached the national newspapers and was widely reported and debated. The Law Society's Journal in the following month posed the intriguing proposition that bigamy among consenting adults should no longer be regarded as a crime.]

DANIEL DOWD

[Editor's note: This is the written testimony of Walter Duckworth in its entirety.]

Daniel Dowd and I were best mates. We were called up together in '39 and reported to the County Barracks. We were lined up with all the other recruits either side of the hall, stripped to the waist with our braces dangling, waiting for the Medical Officer to begin his inspection. The Sergeant Major yelled, "Right, drop your trousers!" We let them fall to our ankles and stood there with our hands coyly cupped over our private parts. I looked across at Dan and got the biggest surprise of my life. He had got the biggest willy I had ever seen. He had his arms folded, not out of bravado but because even if he had tried to hide his bobby dangler with his hands, they would only have covered half. He looked across at me and winked, as if to say, "Well, what do you think of that then?"

We joined the same regiment and went through the war together, finally being demobbed in '46. Shortly after we got back he married Kitty, Kitty Phillips as she then was. I was the best man at his wedding and he at mine.

Kitty was gorgeous, curvaceous and tall, at least four inches taller than Dan, so her choice of Dan as her husband surprised everyone, but not me. All the lads lusted after her, me included, but I knew that no-one could ever compete with Dan in the wedding-tackle stakes. Over the years we met frequently as a foursome until my job took me to Nutchester and we had to move away. Then at the beginning of October last I got a telegram from Kitty telling me that Dan had died. I got leave from work and caught the bus straight to Nutcombe.

Kitty showed me upstairs to where he was lying, and it was there that I got another biggest surprise of my life. Dan had died with an erection which was still there after rigor mortis had set in. He was lying on his back with his over-endowed willy pointing straight up to the ceiling. The sheet covering him looked like an army bell-tent, held aloft by his enormous tent-pole. I exchanged glances with Kitty and she burst into tears.

Just then Lovejoy the undertaker came in with his apprentice, Eric, a bit of a wally, two hinges short of a gate. The school's career master had prevailed upon Lovejoy to take him on because of his qualifications. Qualifications? He'd passed in Religious Instruction and Woodwork, nothing else.

Lovejoy looked at the bell-tent a bit uneasily then strode across and gave the tent-pole a hefty nudge with the heel of his hand. I could tell from his grimace that the jarring had travelled right up his arm. He clearly hadn't expected such stiff opposition. They pulled back the sheet to see exactly what the problem was, and seeing Daniel's naked body they look'd at each other with a wild surmise – silent, upon a peek at Daniel's thighs.

Lovejoy rubbed the muscles of his arm and looked across at his apprentice.

"I think this is a two handed job, Eric. Grab hold of his upright member with me and we'll pull it down when I give the word."

Lovejoy and Eric each grasped the tent-pole with one hand, and at Lovejoy's command they put one foot on the bedstead for greater purchase then strained and puffed away until gradually, degree by degree, they brought it down level to below Daniel's knees. When they looked up from their efforts they saw with astonishment that all had been in vain, for they had merely brought Dan up to the sitting position, and when they released their grip Dan's body gently sank back to where it was before.

Lovejoy was puzzled. The Morticians' Manual was clearly silent on the subject of *rigor mortis erectus* and he stood there silently studying the corpse and fingering his tape-measure. At last he began his measuring.

"Width, OK. Length, OK. Height, Lord give me strength! He'll never fit into any casket we make! Eric, we've got to think of a solution for poor Kitty's sake."

Eric thought. "Let's lay him out proper, but on his side," he said.

"That's merely transferring the bone of contention to another dimension." Lovejoy responded.

Eric thought again. "My sister's a nurse," he said, "and whenever a patient gets a hard-on she gives it a clip with her pencil and it soon goes down."

"I'm sure that would work in cases involving a normal appendage, but even a 4H pencil, which is very hard, would have little effect upon this massive member."

"Why don't we just cut a hole in the lid and let it poke through? We could surround it with flowers to hide it. It could be a floral tribute, in fact."

"A floral tribute?" mused Lovejoy. "Yes, I see what you mean. But supposing the flowers were to fall off? The lady mourners would faint and the men would send cards of sympathy saying 'A Pillar of Strength' or 'Upright to the End' or some such thing."

"We could trim it off to make it level with the lid."

"We'd never match the grain, Eric."

"We could say it was a knot in the wood."

"We are talking about our top of the range caskets, Eric, which never, absolutely never have knots in them!"

Eric was abashed and stood silent for a while, then naughtily said, "Perhaps Mrs Lovejoy could make a suggestion about what to do with the whopping willy in question."

Lovejoy gave him a withering glare.

Just then the Reverend Claud Higgins, vicar of St Barnabas Parish Church, called to pay his respects. On seeing the bell-tent he crossed himself and, searching for a text, said, "And they were even hard at death's door," quoting a passage from Psalm 107 completely out of context.

Lovejoy considered himself a dab hand at quotations and countered with Robert Burns. "All in all, he's a problem must puzzle the devil," he said

The vicar swivelled his head. "Are you saying, M. Lovejoy, that you think that poor Daniel is possessed?"

Lovejoy saw the chance to pass his problem on to Higher Authority. "I'm sure of it, Vicar," he solemnly intoned. "Never have I encountered such a devilish tool."

"My word!" said the vicar, clearly perturbed. "I must arrange a service of exorcism without delay. I must do my duty for my flock who, without exception, have always been as firm as a rock."

The service was arranged and we all trooped into St Barnabas later that day. The service was exceptionally well attended, with some of the lady parishioners vying with each other to be in the front pews. It was only later that the vicar spotted the typing error on the notice-board which stated that Daniel's mighty member was to be exercised.

But the service accomplished nothing. We went back to the house and found the bell-tent still in position. Kitty was beside herself with worry. "What am I going to do, Tess?" she asked her sister.

"I think you should call in a medium," Tessa replied. "Both the vicar and Mr Lovejoy think Daniel is possessed in some way, and I think that might be what's impeding his transfer to the other side."

"But what good is a medium going to do?"

"Well, she could maybe find out whether there was something preying on Daniel's mind."

What Dan's last thoughts were, was there in front of us as plain as a pikestaff. Kitty hesitated but at last agreed, without any hope of a successful outcome, for as everyone knows; a job well done by a medium is rare. So Mrs Wagstaff, the village medium, was sent for. She duly arrived, a pleasant looking woman, aged about forty, a little bit on the plump side, but there's nothing wrong with that on a cold night, I say.

She sat us round the kitchen table with Kitty to her right. The rest of us, Tessa, Lovejoy and Eric, the vicar and me took our nearest place. Mrs Wagstaff told us that she would probably go into a trance, and that if that happened we were to remain completely still and silent until she came out of it.

The séance began. She closed her eyes and soon went into her trance. "How are you, Daniel?" she called out. "Is something bothering you? Kitty is here. Have you a message for her?" There was a pause. Then she suddenly sat up with a start, her eyes opening wide. She closed them again and sat rhythmically swaying for some time, moving her lips as if silently praying. She moaned at times, her plump body heaving, and gasping for air as her breathing raced. Suddenly she flung out her arms as if unable to control herself, then grasping the table she arched her back and let out one final orgasmic scream. With eyes still closed she sat still for a while, her panting gradually easing. Then she rose, straightened her hat and made her way unsteadily towards the front door.

"I'll see myself out, dears," she said, "and there'll be no charge."

"No charge, indeed," cried Tessa. "She didn't do anything!"

But Kitty sensed that some strange force was at play. She jumped up and I followed her as she raced upstairs to where Daniel lay.

The bell-tent had vanished and the tent-pole was down! Kitty wiped away a tear, then smiled, kissed her fingertips and gently laid them upon Dan's smiling lips.

* * *

[Editor's note. Readers may have some difficulty, as I did, in believing this story, but it did gain wide currency at the time. The Nutchester Chronicle published four anonymous poems relating to the event which I found among my grandfather's clippings and now reproduce below.]

Arriving back home still flustered and red,
Mrs Wagstaff turned to her husband and said:
"As you very well know, Alf, I've been a good wife,
But now I need something more out of life.
Today at the séance without any urging,
I felt the free spirit within me surging,
Thus revealing, in spite of your boast,
That you need Viagra[*] more than most."

On their way back to the Chapel of Rest
Lovejoy had something to get off his chest.
He turned to his young apprentice and said:
"You know, Eric, a thought has just entered my head.
The art of the medium, over centuries imparted,
Is raising the spirit of one dear departed;
But when there are unquenched passions to quell,
Mrs Wagstaff can lower the flesh as well."

That night as the vicar lay back in his bed
He turned to his pretty young wife and said:
"I know that mediums can produce ectoplasm,
But today I saw one achieve ecto-orgasm."
"You obviously believe it was genuine, I take it,
But can you be sure she didn't just fake it?"
"Oh no, dear, or else I'd have seen right through it."
"Really?" thought Joyce. "Well, I sometimes do it."

As Tessa was putting her case in the car
To journey back home to Leamington Spa
She turned to her sister, Kitty, and said:
"How will you cope now that Daniel is dead?"
"I know I'll have setbacks as never before,
But I'll keep his example well to the fore.
The harder things get, with Dan's inspiration,
I'll rise, just like he did, to every occasion."

* * *

* [The actual words in the newspaper cutting were 'Monkey glands' which were the then current presumed sexual aid, but I have substituted 'Viagra' for the benefit of modern readers.]

SID'S REVENGE

Sid Pollifax had almost finished cleaning the upstairs windows when his wife called.

"SidNEY! Haven't you finished yet? My ladies will be here shortly and I don't want you getting in the way. Finish what you're doing then go and sit in the shed until four o'clock, and then you can bring in our tea and cakes! And for goodness sake don't shuffle when you bring them in!"

"Alright, dear," answered Sid resignedly.

How different it all had been, forty years ago, when they first were married. He had been the squire's groom, earning Colonel Buckmaster's respect over the years. To the squire's family's relief, and with their whole-hearted blessing, he had married the squire's bizarre and headstrong niece, Hermione, and with his approval he had volunteered for the army amid the patriotic fervour of 1914. His army career proved to be short-lived, however, for in April 1915 he had been wounded and gassed near Ypres and was invalided out, a changed and broken man. His wife was unprepared for the change in their fortunes and begged of the family to be relieved somehow of the burden. The squire had sternly reminded her of her wedding vows – for richer, for poorer, in sickness and in health, - and would hear none of it.

Although Sid was no longer fit enough to work as a groom, the squire was proud of his ex-employee and settled him and his niece in one of the estate's houses as joint tenants at a peppercorn rent, and made them a generous joint allowance. Hermione, however, was far from proud of her husband and saw the social whirl she had always imagined for herself now crumbled into dust. Were it not for the squire's generosity which bound them together for life, she would have discarded Sid long ago. Instead, in her bitterness, she had set about making his life a misery. Since he was no longer fit enough to do a man's work, she decided he should do a woman's work instead - her own, to be precise. She had listed all the chores to be done throughout the house and entered them on worksheets, day by day, hour by hour. She checked the work he did and if he fell short in any degree she lambasted him with fury.

Sid was seething inwardly. "My ladies will be here shortly," he mimicked sarcastically to himself. "They're all as twisted as she is. Frauds, the lot of them." For his wife fancied herself as a medium and had built up a coterie of like-minded friends who attended her séances frequently. In this she was encouraged by Mrs Eustacia Crabbe who had spotted the fraud early on and had decided to get into the act. Years before when Sid's wife was in one of her trances, and claimed to be in contact with her spirit guide, Mrs Crabbe had called out, "I can see her! I can see Princess Moolaaba." She then described in such fine detail the dress and appearance of the princess of unspecified nationality that Sid's wife was compelled to confirm that, yes, it was the very one. Thereafter, acting as a pair, they were able to convince the gullible of their psychic powers.

It was all a fraud, as Sid said. He could guess the result of the phoney séances. He had heard them so many times before. Mrs Crabbe would already have made enquiries about any new member and passed this information to his wife so that the newcomer would be amazed at the medium's prescience. What amazed Sid was the fact that his wife had come to believe she really did possess psychic powers.

As instructed, he put down his duster and went to the garden shed, but he did not go in. Instead he went out of the garden through the side gate and along the lane which led to the Red Lion. He entered the Public Bar, ordered his pint of ale and took it over to the bench. There he sat down, opened an exercise book, licked the stub end of his pencil and put a tick against three items.

Ron Baker, the pub manager, called across to him. "That's the morning done, is it, Sid? What's on for this afternoon?"

Sid consulted the exercise book. "Thursday p.m.," he said. "Oh, it's not too bad. Dust banisters, straighten rugs, polish table top. That's all. I can fit those in nicely, and with a bit of luck I'll avoid the sharp end of her tongue."

Ron shook his head as if in disbelief, for Sid's henpecked life was common knowledge throughout the village. What was not so widely known, however, was the fact that on the evenings when his wife went out, and there were many of them - W.I., bridge circles and the like - Sid would slip away to Dolly Peaslake's cottage to spend a pleasant hour or two in her company. Their affair had begun in 1918, soon after Dolly had received a telegram saying that her husband, Ted, would not be returning from the war. From its passionate beginnings their relationship had gradually developed into a loving, comfortable companionship which each of them wore like a favourite jacket.

Sid was about to lift his glass when he felt a sudden pain. He stood up unsteadily and gasped, "Ron!" then slumped forward across the table. Ron called Dr Kendall from across the street, who examined Sid and pronounced him dead.

"It's his heart," he said. "I'm surprised he's lasted this long."

They sent for Mr Lovejoy, the undertaker, who conveyed Sid's body to the Chapel of Rest at the rear of his funeral parlour.

The Parish Church was filled to overflowing at Sid's funeral service, with the Rev. Claud Higgins making a sincere and touching funeral oration. As his coffin was lowered into the ground the mourners facing Sid's wife were shocked to see the smile on her face.

Four days later the villagers assembled once again, this time in the Village Hall at the request of Sid's solicitors, Flint, Flint and Flint. The vicar called the meeting to order and Mr Flint (the middle one) rose to make his announcement.

"On the instructions of my late client, Mr Sidney Pollifax, his will is to be read in public in the Village Hall before assembled villagers. It is a short document, in verse but valid nonetheless, so I shall read it out in full." He cleared his throat and read:

"Dear heartless wife, For what it's worth,
You made my life a hell on earth.
But nonetheless I leave to you
All I possess, the work-sheets, too.
But first, there's something you should know;
That at our bank, some time ago,
I drew out all our cash, the lot,
And in some safe secluded spot
I buried it. But never fear,
Here's how to get it back, my dear.
Take my work-sheets - though now they're yours -
And every day do all the chores
Which you yourself said must be done.
So do them all - yes, every one -
And properly, mind! I'll have no botching!
Remember always I'll be watching!

When you've done that for one whole year
Just contact me, I'm bound to hear.
I'll tell you then just where it's hid.
'Til then, bye bye,
Yours truly,
Sid."

    Immediately, the hall was filled with spontaneous, riotous laughter, villagers laughing, hugging, whistling and stamping their feet. It was extremely unseemly – but immensely enjoyable, for the villagers' sorrow for Sid had evaporated in that instant and for ever after their memory of him would be a happy one.

    The months passed in succession, with Sid's wife beavering away through the worksheets. At the end of the year, in accordance with Sid's will, she tried desperately but unsuccessfully to contact him. Professional pride prevented her from seeking help from Mrs Wagstaff, the medium whose powers were so clearly demonstrated by the Daniel Dowd affair, so eventually and reluctantly Hermione conceded that her psychic powers fell short of the requirements.

    It was then that Dolly Peaslake put on her wellington boots and went into her garden. She took a spade from the shed and started to dig at the spot which Sid had pointed out to her, until she heard a metallic click. She scooped out more soil with her hands, lifted the cash box out, filled the hole in again and went back indoors. She later moved away from Nutcombe and bought River Cottage in Felsham, but every Monday she catches the bus back in order to renew the flowers on Sid's grave in the Parish Churchyard.

* * *

THE WATER CRISIS

The summer had been hot and long, the sort that had children playing and tempers fraying. In late May the Nutchester Chronicle displayed the headline, "Phew! What a Scorcher!" accompanied by a photograph of an egg frying on the pavement. In June the headline was, "Heat-wave Continues!" and the photograph was of an egg and two rashers of bacon. In July the headline was, "When Will it End?" and only the intervention of the proprietors prevented the publication of a photograph displaying a full English breakfast.

By August everyone was aware that the situation was serious. Following a dry winter, the reservoirs were at their lowest recorded level, and in Nutchester the authorities were making provision for stand-pipes in the street. There were appeals for the public to use water sparingly, to use the bath water more than once and not drain it away. Some took this an encouragement for couples to bath together, which made the County Registrar revise his population growth estimates upwards. Other restrictions were put in place, though the greens at the Nutchester Bowls Club continued to be maintained in pristine condition. Suggestions that this was due to the number of City Councillors who were members of the Club were rejected by them as ill-informed calumny.

The water supply for the village of Nutcombe was via a reservoir tank buried deep in the hills above the village and the gauges showed that the level was becoming perilously low. Action clearly had to be taken so an extraordinary meeting of the Rural District Council was called to debate the matter. Alderman Charles Fetlock occupied the Chair and called the meeting to order. There were some who immediately questioned whether any amount of talking could alter the fact that the County was subject to the forces of nature. They argued that if talking could produce rain then previous Council Meetings should have flooded the Nutt Valley many times over. The debate had lasted well into the evening, with no progress having been made, when Cllr. Alf Watney rose to make a serious suggestion. The other members should have known from past experience that Alf's suggestions ran the entire gamut of intelligence from down-right crazy to absolutely stupid. It was he who had suggested a solution to an 80 foot radio mast needed for the RAF wireless station at Nutcombe Priory during the war. Some villagers had worried that the mast would spoil the view and the scenic beauty of the area. Alf had seen no problem at all. "The solution is simple," he had said. "We should sink a shaft 80 feet into the ground to house the mast, and then no-one would notice it at all!"

They should have remembered, but they were tired and anxious to get home. Alf rose. "Gentlemen," he said, "The solution is simple. The obvious way to counter the water shortage and to make it go further is to dilute it at source!"

The suggestion galvanized the meeting and there were many objections. "I cannot agree," said Cllr. Phipps. "Weaker water would mean we would all have to use twice the number of tea-bags to get the same cup of tea, and what with the price of tea being what it is it's not on."

Cllr. Potts raised the question of safety. "Weaker water would seriously alter the buoyancy of the village swimming pool, but who can tell in which direction? Only the first drowning would answer that question."

"Will our water-rates be halved?" asked Cllr. Crankshaft. "They should be if the water's only half-strength."

"I pay for the water I use on my small-holding by meter," moaned Cllr. Whelks. "The question is, will it then go at twice the speed or only half?"

"Whichever it is you can be sure you'll be paying more!" said a wag.

"Gentlemen! Gentlemen!" Alderman Fetlock pleaded. "We're getting nowhere. I suggest we adopt the proposal and pass it on to the Engineering Department for their evaluation. All those in favour? Right. Meeting closed. Let's get home."

The news of the meeting leaked out to the villagers who set about stocking up, using whatever utensils they could, to store water before it was reduced in strength. One commercially-minded lady seized upon the opportunity to profit from the news. Miss Betty divided the bottled water on her shelves in her corner shop, labelling one section "Full Strength" and added a ha'penny to the price.

The vicar, the Rev. Claud Higgins, was gravely concerned about the water for the font. Everybody knew, of course, that it did not come from the River Jordan but was supplied somehow by the Nutt Valley Water Authority through the tap on the wall of the north transept, and it was assumed by all that Higher Authority had sanctioned this downgrading. But, wondered the vicar, what would that Higher Authority think about baptisms performed with diluted water? It was not a matter upon which he felt competent to judge, so he sat down and wrote a letter to Bishop Bob, his uncle, seeking guidance.

In the Red Lion the arguments nearly came to blows. Some customers sought guarantees that their beer would never be made with diluted water, while others said that they had always assumed that Ron Baker watered his beer, anyway.

"Yes!" cried one. "But that is with full-strength water. We don't want him to do it with diluted."

Ron was furious. "Look here!" he cried. "I've never watered the beer here at any time, and I've got the hydrometer readings to prove it."

"Ah", said another. "That's a point. Will we be able to rely upon those readings in future?"

Ron's wife, Betty, spoke up. "I don't see what you're worried about. If the brewery does start using diluted water you'll be able to drink twice as much before getting drunk."

"Yeah, maybe. But I bet you won't be reducing the price, will you?"

*

The stockpiling of water by the villagers completely emptied the tank and the County Council was forced to send a water-bowser to the village. News of this development alarmed the villagers and a rumour spread like wildfire that they were going to be forced to drink diluted water. The bowser was spotted as it passed through Little Parsley and the news was flashed through to Nutcombe where barricades had been erected at the crossroads. There the bowser was brought to a standstill by red-faced and determined citizens bearing banners reading, "Death before Dilution!", "We say No! to your H_2O", and "Full Strength and no Butts."

The driver of the bowser stepped from his cab and approached the crowd.

"What's going on?" he asked, raising his cap to scratch his head. "We're bringing water to Nutcombe. Don't you want it?"

"Not if it's diluted," they cried.

"It's water, for Pete's sake!" he cried, exasperated.

"Yes, but is it diluted?" they asked.

"Of course not! It's just pure water."

"How do we know it's not diluted?"

"What's wrong with you people? It's water. You can't dilute water."

"Don't think you can fool us with your fancy talk. We need to be convinced you're not tricking us."

"Yes! Someone go and fetch Ron's hydrometer," the carrier of the H_2O banner shouted.

Billy Enright sped off on his bicycle and returned with Ron and his hydrometer.

"Let's test it!" they cried.

The driver resignedly took a mug from his cab, went to the rear of the bowser, turned the cock so that water dribbled out and filled the mug. He passed it to Ron who floated his hydrometer in the liquid.

"What does it read, Ron?" they asked.

Ron peered at the slender stem and checked. "Eleven percent proof," he said.

"Eleven percent proof!" the male villagers cried. "That's the same as wine! Let the bowser through! Let it through!"

The driver turned to his mate with eyes lifted in disbelief. "They're barmy, Sid! Plain barmy!"

"I expect they're dehydrated, Charlie, that's all."

The bowser made its way into Nutcombe and stopped in the square. The menfolk and their wives rushed indoors and collected the utensils they had previously filled. They emptied that water away down the sink or the drain and queued up to have them re-filled with the eleven percent proof variety.

*

Meanwhile in Nutchester the atmosphere was oppressive. Since early morning the air had been sultry and still. Inside the

Bishop's Palace the Reverend Desmond Bland, the bishop's secretary, limped in to the Bishop's office with the mail. "There's a letter from your nephew in Nutcombe, my lord."

Bishop Bob moved away from the open window where he had been hoping to breathe what little cool air there was, and read Claud's letter. "Dear God," he cried, "Please get those mad, mad parishioners off my back!"

At that moment the curtains began to stir and a breeze was suddenly whipped up. There was a flash of lightning and the windows rattled as a thunder-clap reverberated across the city. The heavens opened and the rain poured down in continuous sheets. The Bishop closed the window hurriedly, looked at his secretary and smiled.

"My word, Desmond," he said, "I have never before received such an immediate response."

The rain did not abate until three days had passed. It poured down the baked hillsides into the streams and rivers and then into the reservoirs. The long hot summer had ended and the seasonal autumn rains returned.

* * *

[Editor's note: The water crisis is now largely forgotten in Nutchester, but the sense of the occasion is preserved by the Nutcombe museum which displays three bottles of water, one labelled 'diluted', one 'full strength' and the third 'eleven percent proof'. The card beneath the exhibits reads, "On loan from Miss Betty's Corner Shop, open daily 8 a.m. to 6 p.m."]

DAISY DIMPLE

A few months after his trial for bigamy, Peter Penny cycled back to Nutcombe, turning left at the crossroads, making it clear to the villagers that he was returning from a night spent with Elsie, his Gifford wife. He cycled past the garage and turned into the lane leading to his cottage and his smithy. He rested his bike against his cottage porch and went inside to the welcoming warmth and the smell of coffee and newly baked bread. His Nutcombe wife, Peggy, was in the kitchen preparing breakfast.

"Morning, Pet," she greeted him. "And how is Elsie?"

"She's grand, Peggy, and sends her love."

"That's nice. And how's young Simon coming along?"

"He's learning fast," Peter enthused. "I have great hopes for him."

"You're a good father to him, to be sure. Now, did you have breakfast there? If not I'll do some for you now. No? Right, you get the brazier started in the forge and I'll have something on the table for you by the time you get back."

When Peter returned he sat down to a plate piled high with eggs, ham and sautéed potatoes, and tucked in with gusto, needing strength for the heavy day ahead. Peggy sat at the table opposite him.

"Daisy was asking for you yesterday evening," she said.

"Daisy? Daisy who?"

"Daisy Dimple, 36,28,34, the one who won the beauty contest a few years back."

"Oh her! So what did she want?"

"She didn't say, but she said it was important. I told her as like as not you'd be in the Red Lion this lunch time and could possibly see her then."

"That's what I'll do then," Peter said, "though Lord knows what she could want with me."

Peggy rose and stood in front of him with arms folded. "Well," she said, "if she's wanting to be your next wife I'll tell you right now, Peter Penny, that it won't get my approval, and I'm sure that goes for the others, too. She's no better than she should be, that girl!"

*

The Red Lion was busy that lunchtime, but Peter had managed to sit at his usual place in the corner, away from the workers who crowded the bar. He had finished his meat pie and was about to relax with his pipe when Daisy entered. She looked around, saw Peter, and walked purposefully towards him.

"Hello, Mr Penny," she said. "Did Peggy tell you I would like a word with you?"

"Yes, lass, she did. And call me Peter." He indicated the chair as he pulled it away from the table and said, "Won't you sit down?" As she settled down Peter appraised her appearance. She was a good-looker, the right side of thirty he guessed, and a bit plumper than when she won the beauty contest, but still attractive, nonetheless. "What was it you wanted to see me about?"

She looked him straight in the eye and said almost in defiance, "You know I entertain several gentlemen friends, I suppose?"

"Aye, lass, so I've heard."

"Well, now I'm in a spot of bother with one of them. Well, not really one of them, but a casual one-off customer."

"What sort of bother?" he asked, wondering if she wanted him to sort someone out.

"I'd better tell you everything from the beginning," Daisy said, "especially if you're going to represent me."

Peter filled his pipe slowly to give himself time to consider the implications of that final remark. "Go on, lass," he said at last.

Daisy recounted her tale. "One evening two weeks ago I was in here with Eugenie Lascelles, the one who runs the beauty salon. I wasn't looking for business, just having a quiet drink with a friend. There was a chap staying here at the Red Lion. He was stood by the bar and he kept eyeing me like he was wondering what his chances were. I didn't fancy him much. He was only a year or two away from being a dirty old man, if you know what I mean. Anyway, he eventually plucked up courage and walked across to our table. Eugenie could see it was business so she said goodnight and left. This chap came up and said, 'How much?' I was flabbergasted. Normally they ask you if you'd like a drink, chat you up and talk for a bit. But he just said, 'How much?' just like that. For a moment I thought of saying, 'Piss off!' and wish I had done now, but business is business, so I upped my price and said, '£10!' 'Right,' he said. 'Let's go.'

"I took him home and got my kit off ready for him. I watched as he took off his trousers and could hardly stop myself from laughing. His little cock was hanging down, looking just like a shrivelled up old carrot, and I remember thinking he'll never get that up. I was right, he never did. I did all I could to get an erection for him but it was hopeless. He was cussing and muttering and then eventually he gave up. He dressed himself and made for the door. 'Hey!' I said. 'What about my £10?' 'Get stuffed!' he cried. 'Not by you I couldn't!' I shouted after him. Well, that was that. I couldn't go back to the pub because he was staying there, and if I'd kicked up a row there that wouldn't have done Ron's business any good, nor mine, so I stayed at home fuming for the rest of the evening."

Peter was now dreading that Daisy was about to ask him to dust this fellow up. He was big enough and strong enough to do it, but it really wasn't his scene. "I'm sorry, Daisy," he said. "I'm afraid I'm not going to be able to help you."

"No, no, wait! I haven't finished yet. As I was saying, I was furious that a working girl could be done out of her money with impunity like that, so I decided something had to be done about it. I had a look at the register of the Red Lion and found out who he was. His name was Richard Small, a commercial traveller from Wheskers in Cranbury. I had to laugh when I saw that. Dick Small! His mother must have guessed what was what when she christened him. Anyway, next day I went to Flint, Flint and Flint, solicitors, to see about suing him. I told Mr Flint, the middle one, what had happened and he said, 'You can't sue him because it's ex-terpsichore' or something like that. Terpsichore is dancing, ain it? I didn't do any dancing, honest. I wiggled my hips a bit to try to get him a hard-on, but I didn't do any dancing. Anyway, that was what he said - I couldn't sue him. I'm sure he was wrong, but he charged me two and a half guineas just the same. I was going to forget about it all, when I thought of you and your trial and how you had been able to prove the Law wrong, and I thought perhaps with your legal knowledge you could help me get my money back."

Peter felt immensely relieved. It was his brain she wanted, not his brawn. He recalled the words she had used – 'especially if you're going to represent me'. Represent me, that's what she'd said. The blacksmith's chest swelled with pride. He remembered his moment in the magistrate's court when he'd argued his own case to a successful conclusion. And now - to be asked to represent someone! His thoughts raced on, so that Daisy became worried by his silence. She thought she needed to strengthen her appeal, so she pulled at her satin blouse to make it fit the tighter and took in a deep, cleavage-enhancing breath.

"I'd be very grateful, Peter," she said, placing her hand upon one of his. "Extremely grateful."

Peter came back to earth. "Now now lass," he said. "That's enough of that. Delightful as I'm sure that would be, I must resist the temptation. I'm a married man and faithful to all my wives. But I will take your case on, for the challenge."

In due course Peter took the bus to Nutchester library and surrounded himself with law books. He began his study of them and soon received a nasty shock, for the solicitor had been right. Daisy could not sue, and it had nothing to do with Terpsichore. The phrase that Mr Flint had used was *ex turpi causa*, the legal maxim that the courts will not allow an action on a contract containing an illegal or immoral element. For a time he sat there, utterly defeated, the chance of representing someone in court evaporating like the steam when a red-hot horseshoe is plunged into cold water. But his resolution returned when he thought of his own trial and how he had found the solution in *mens rea*. Perhaps if he delved deeper he would discover the means that would enable the law to come to the aid of an honest working girl. Thus fortified he carried on his research, until, hours later, he caught the bus back to Nutcombe, there to pen his missive to the judge at the County Court in Nutchester, confident that once more he had found the means to confound the Law.

*

His Honour Judge Archibald Browne read through his correspondence of the day and eventually came to Peter's letter. He read it with astonishment then burst out laughing. He looked at the signature "Peter Penny (blacksmith)" and laughed again. Then he picked up the phone and dialled the number of his friend, Mr Montague Middleton, the Stipendiary Magistrate, whose office in the Magistrates Court was on the opposite side of Market Square to the County Court. "Hello, Monty," he said. "I've got something here which will amuse you. Can you come across sometime?"

"I can come across now, Archie, if it won't take long," Mr Middleton replied, and so made his way to the Judge's chambers.

The Judge handed him Peter's letter saying, "You'll love this."

Mr Middleton read:

"Dear Judge,

I represent Miss Daisy Dimple and wish to sue Richard Small for the recovery of a debt amounting to the sum of £10. Will you please put the necessary procedures in train and let me know the date of the trial. I remain,

Yours faithfully
Peter Penny (blacksmith)."

"Well, what do you think of that, Monty?" the Judge asked. "Your blacksmith obviously thinks he's God's answer to the legal profession, yet clearly knows absolutely nothing about court procedure."

"Just about the same as we know about shoeing horses, I should think," responded the magistrate sagely.

"True, true, very true. But I mean to say.... Anyway, I thought I'd let you see it before I threw it in the bin."

"No, don't do that. The blacksmith's a good man and well regarded in Nutcombe. And in the surrounding villages," he added with a laugh.

"Well, I can't act upon the letter, Monty. You know that. We can't have a case involving £10 in the County Court. It would be *de minimis*. Doesn't the fellow know he isn't qualified anyway to represent anybody?"

Montague Middleton was deep in thought. He had a sneaking regard for Peter Penny and admired the simple honesty which shone through his letter. Though it was often said that ignorance of the law is no defence, neither, he thought, is it a cause for shame. Daisy Dimple had a debt owing to her, and the blacksmith was anxious that she should recover it. The Law should help them, not reject their cause because of its relative smallness. There were times, he remembered, when £10 had meant a very great deal to him. Filled with resolve he faced his friend.

"Archie," he began, "What would you say if I asked you to let me deal with this in the Lower Court?"

"A civil debt recovery case in the Magistrates Court? That's a bit unusual, isn't it?"

"I would do it informally, a sort of arbitration but with the full force of the law behind my decision, just as it would be if the case were heard in the County Court. What do you say?"

Archibald Browne pondered a while and then agreed. "Alright, Monty, if that's what you wish, though if it were me, I'd take £10 from my own wallet and give it to the blacksmith so that I could stick to the normal procedures I'm happy with."

*

Mr Middleton wrote to Peter Penny requesting formal details of the parties, obtained their consent to his proposal and then issued summonses for them to appear before him at the Magistrates Court in Nutchester on the appointed day. Daisy was represented by Peter, and Richard Small was represented by Ephraim Flint, the middle one. The court rose as Mr Middleton entered to take his seat on the Bench. He looked across at Peter.

"Ah, Mr Penny," he said. "And how are your wives?"

"They're all very well, your honour, and thank you kindly for asking."

"And I take it that it is only Miss Dimple you are representing, and that there won't be four others I would need to take into account?"

Peter smiled and replied, "No, just the one, your honour."

"That's fine. I just wanted to be sure of what I was facing. Well, Mr Penny, let's hear your submission. To begin with I'd like to know the nature of Miss Dimple's debt."

"It's for personal services, your honour."

"What sort of personal services were they?"

"Very personal, your honour."

Mr Middleton started in his chair. "Do I understand that Miss Dimple is a prostitute?"

"More of a good-time girl, your honour. She doesn't solicit business."

"You are wasting the court's time, Mr Penny. You cannot bring a case involving immorality because *ex turpi causa*......"

".... *non oritur actio*" interjected Peter. "I do know what the term means, your honour, and hope to demonstrate to the court that the maxim does not apply in the present case."

Mr Middleton tried hard to disguise his amusement at the brass cheek of the fellow. He knew full well that the maxim would eventually apply and that in the end he would have to dismiss Daisy Dimple's claim, but until then he thought he would let the blacksmith present his spurious argument and enjoy it. "Do then proceed," he said.

Peter began. "Prostitution is the act of performing sexual activity......"

".... in exchange for money or goods," interjected Middleton. "I do know what the term means, Penny, but please do continue."

Peter then repeated to the court all that Daisy had told him, of the agreement for £10, of Daisy's efforts to fulfil her part of the contract, of the inability of the shrivelled carrot to grow as Nature intended, and of Richard Small's refusal to pay. "So you see, your honour," he concluded, "no sexual activity actually occurred and no money changed hands. The most that can be said is that it was *attempted* prostitution, and while prostitution is covered by the maxim, *attempted* prostitution is not mentioned at all. Nor can I find any reference to it in any of the law books or reported cases. This being so, one must conclude that the legislators and judges did not have it in mind to include it in their strictures. Thus we are left with a case of contract law, pure and simple."

Mr Middleton chuckled to himself and, warming to the scene, decided to play along with it. "Since your client performed her part of the bargain insofar as she was able," he said, "are you claiming on a *quantum meruit* basis, Mr Penny?"

"No, your honour. Our claim is for an agreed amount and not for an unliquidated sum. Furthermore, claiming on *quantum meruit* would entail evaluating the various stages of my client's services, a task well beyond the expertise of any quantity surveyor. Besides which, we are also claiming for damages, which in itself rules out a *quantum meruit* claim."

Mr Middleton, impressed by the blacksmith's grasp of the subject, nodded his acceptance of Peter's position and turned to Richard Small's solicitor.

"Well, Mr Flint," he said, "You have heard Penny's submission. Do you wish to contest any substantial statement of fact?"

Mr Flint rose and with a high-pitched and tinny voice replied, "We accept that the facts as cited are basically correct apart from the reference to 'a shrivelled up old carrot' which my client vehemently denies."

"Well, as you therefore accept that a contract existed, what reasons are you putting forward for your client's refusal to pay?"

"Frustration, your honour. Frustration pure and simple, brought about by both impossibility and the non-occurrence of an event."

Mr Middleton was not impressed with the answer. "The parties may have been frustrated, Flint, but the contract certainly was not. The impossibility to perform was due to your client's impotence, which led to the non-occurrence of an event which itself was the subject matter of the contract. Have you no better argument?"

"Act of God, your honour. My client was ready and willing to perform, but unable to do so due to the physical limits which his Maker had imposed upon him."

"Really, Mr Flint! If that were a valid defence no-one would be responsible for anything. Have you no other defence to put forward?"

Mr Flint and Richard Small had already agreed upon a fall-back position which would delay and could possibly thwart the action indefinitely. He cleared his throat and continued with a high-pitched whine, "Since the court has been pleased not to accept the previous defences, as a sincere gesture of good-will my client is willing to perform his obligations under the contract at a time and place mutually to be agreed between the parties."

This announcement took the court by surprise. Mr Middleton turned towards Peter. "What response does your client wish to make to this proposal, Mr Penny?"

The blacksmith bent towards Daisy and entered into a whispered conversation. "Well, what do you think, lass? Are you prepared to let him have another try?"

"I don't want to," she declared. "I've already had my kit off for him once. And what if he can't get it up again? We'd all be back here again in a couple of months' time."

"That's a good point!" said Peter. After turning it over in his mind he turned to address the court. "Your honour, Mr Flint knows full well that the original contract no longer exists. It was repudiated by his client's refusal to pay. What is being suggested now is a new contract based loosely on the terms of the old one. Before my client could even consider entering into it, bearing in mind her past experience with Mr Small, she would wish to be certain of his ability to carry out its terms, and would seek a guarantee of performance backed by suitable penalty clauses. Otherwise we will all be back here sometime in the future arguing the same points again."

Mr Middleton nodded, turned to Mr Flint and asked, "What is your response to that, Mr Flint?"

There was a hurried conversation between solicitor and client, in which it was clear that Mr Small was in no way certain of his ability to achieve an erection on demand. Mr Flint eventually addressed the court again.

"We cannot accept that stipulation, your honour. My client has shown his utmost willingness to settle this dispute, but if circumstances are such that he is unable to perform again, that should be the end of the matter. If that proves to be the position both parties should accept that the terms of the contract have been carried out in full."

"Are you saying, Mr Flint," asked the magistrate, "that at that point both parties should accept that the contract in all its terms should be deemed to have been fulfilled, both parties having carried out their obligations?"

"Exactly so, your honour."

"But Mr Flint, that was exactly the position facing your client when he refused to pay before. Due to that damning admission I have no hesitation now in finding for Miss Dimple."

He turned to Peter and said, "I gather you are seeking damages, Mr Penny. May I ask on what grounds?"

"Damage to my client's reputation, your honour."

"Her reputation? How on earth has that been damaged?"

"Well, as your honour can see, she is a very attractive lady, but Mr Small's refusal to pay could leave one to surmise that those attractions are not worth paying for. Further, his impotence in her presence could leave one to surmise that there must be some dark and sinister factor about her being which drives all thought of sex from a man's mind. Any future gentleman friend could therefore avoid her companionship for fear of experiencing *reductio ad absurdum*, or worse still of becoming impotent. All this is damaging to my client's interest and is worthy of compensation."

"I see, Mr Penny. And what quantum of damages do you have in mind?"

"Twenty pounds should cover it, your honour."

"So awarded. Now, to sum up and for the record, I find for Miss Dimple in the matter of the debt and additionally award her damages in the sum of £20 to cover potential damage to her reputation."

He leant across for his gavel to bring the proceedings to an end, when Peter sprang to his feet.

"And the costs, your honour?"

Mr Middleton smiled. "Yes, and costs, Mr Penny."

*

The street lights were beginning to go on as Daisy and Peter, nearly £50 to the good, boarded the bus back to Nutcombe. For most of the journey they laughed and revelled in their success in court, but as the bus wound its way through the villages they fell strangely silent. When they neared Nutcombe, Daisy placed her hand high up on the inside of Peter's leg and softly said, "Your wives need never know, Peter."

* * *

[Editor's note: From my grandfather's cuttings I saw that this case was featured on the front page of the Nutchester Chronicle under the headline **LOCAL BLACKSMITH STRIKES AGAIN** and was picked up by the national newspapers. In some legal circles *Dimple v Small* is cited as being influential in the creation of the small claims procedure which was formally introduced into the English court system in 1973.]

THE ARSONIST

[Editor's note: Among my grandfather's papers was a yellowed press cutting of Reg v Sly, a criminal case which he had covered for the Nutchester Chronical, together with a copy of the Autumn 1957 edition of the Nutt Valley Quarterly which contained the following poem submitted by "F.G.S.", my grandfather's initials. I had no idea that he had had a poetical bent and now suspect that it was he who had penned the verses following the Daniel Dowd affair. However, here is the poem.]

*

This is the tale of Jasper Sly,
A seemingly unlucky guy,
Who nonetheless was unperturbed
By the fires which oft occurred
Destroying all the furs and gowns
He held in stock in various towns;
For after each successive claim
It seemed the richer he became.

For instance, he was on a cruise
When they broke to him the dreadful news;
But on returning from his hols
He bought himself a brand new Rolls.
Another time he wept aloud
As the Fire Brigade kept back the crowd;
But his smile was bright and his eyes were dry
When he bought more shares in ICI.

His house in Nutcombe Heights, though brash,
Was bought entirely with the cash
Donated by the Pearl, the Pru,
Lloyd's, Sun Alliance and NFU.
But Jasper erred in tempting Fate
Which unbeknown had fixed the date
This arsonist of rag-trade premises
Would meet, unrecognized, his Nemesis.

So enters Percy, a genial soul,
Who chose to supplement his dole
By working as a part-time barman,
Roofer, cleaner, labourer, carman,
Receiving as his normal fee
Cash in hand and all tax-free,
Income he'd have not enjoyed
Were he not fully unemployed.

His many skills he advertised
On bits of paper, post-card sized,
Which dear Miss Betty did display
In her corner shop window, a penny a day.
"Experienced roofer. Terms agreed.
Satisfaction guaranteed.
If your garage roof's a'leaking
I'm the craftsman you are seeking."

And so it was, as if by chance,
That Jasper gave that ad a glance,
And as the rain *was* coming through
His garage roof, without ado
He phoned to Percy who agreed
To do the job with utmost speed.
So mid-way through the following week
Percy arrived to tackle the leak.

After off-loading the burner and felt
And waiting around for the asphalt to melt,
He then read the Herald and finished a fag
By which time his energy had started to flag.
Deciding the cause was his need for some grub
He climbed into his van and drove off to Ron's pub;
There to indulge in the food he loved most -
Baked beans piled high upon pieces of toast.

His predilection for baked beans,
Acquired while he was in his teens,
This day was pre-ordained to be
The cause of untold misery;
For instead of being grateful
For a single piled-high plateful
He to the busy barman beckoned
And rashly ordered up a second;

Then proceeding a la carte
Devoured a wedge of rhubarb tart,
And brought his repast to a finish
By downing yet another Guinness.
His far from balanced meal now ended
He drove to Jasper's, stomach distended,
And as the afternoon progressed
Became increasingly distressed.

He could not work with belly so bloated
Nor with the discomfort this promoted,
And soon the rumblings in his tum
Convinced him that the time had come
To seek de-pressurized relief;
So, tensing his muscles and clenching his teeth,
By a prolonged but natural function
He purged the product of his gaseous luncheon.

This methane, searching for the air,
Found an outlet nearby where
His trusty blow-torch stood alight
Which caused the methane to ignite.
The flame pursued its natural course
And journeyed swiftly to the source,
Thereby scorching, inter alia,
His unsuspecting genitalia.

Poor Percy doubled up with pain,
Which caused him to break wind again,
So unwittingly infringing
The patent for a two-stroke engine.
As the flames took hold he could not bear
Such novel thermal underwear,
So now with trousers well alight
He vainly sought relief in flight.

Into the house he headlong rushed,
His cheeks by now both hotly flushed,
And in his mind a single thought - t'
Plunge his bum in cooling water.
Flinging wide the kitchen door
He saw arranged upon the floor
Some thinners stored in pots and pans
All part of Jasper's future plans.

Believing it was H_2O
He sat in one, which in a mo
Converted his ill-judged compulsion
Into a form of jet-propulsion.
For now like a doodle-bug he flew,
Through the ceiling, past the loo,
Defying laws once held inviolate
As, flying blind on auto pilot,

He blazed along the upstairs landing,
Then, stud-partition notwithstanding,
Crashed through into the master bedroom
Which, by virtue of its vaster headroom,
Allowed his progress aerobatic
To proceed unhindered t'wards the attic,
Ever onwards and upwards hurtling,
Till brought to rest by a timber purlin.

Alas, poor Percy's now departed,
Leaving kinfolk broken-hearted,
Unable fully to comprehend
How he came to have such a fiery end.

The net result of Percy's flight
Was to set Jasper's house alight,
In the process leaving traces
Of thinners in unlikely places,
A fact which those with expertise
Could spot with unaccustomed ease.
A fact which also, at a guess,
Could lead to charges - but I digress.

The scene now shifts to Felsham Road
Where Jasper had started to unload
Some cotton waste he planned to use
As a tried and trusted fuse,
When down the road with bell a'ringing
A police patrol car came a'winging,
And from John Banks our Jasper learned
That his house at Nutcombe Heights had burned.

This news invoked surprise, and sorrow,
For the fire was not until the morrow,
And not at his own private dwelling
But at his shop where the clothes weren't selling.
For a moment he stood there, stunned,
Mobile features moribund.
Then, unaware of Percy's fate
He started to expostulate.

"The roofer did it! God, he's dim!
I take it you have questioned him?"
"I cannot, sir, and I'll tell you why –
He's joined the dole queue in the sky.
But it was not him, and that's a fact,
For the garage roof is still intact.
No, this fire was started flagrantly
And caused by human agency.

"Which brings me to my own pet theory,
Prompting an initial query.
Can I ask you, for beginners,
Just why you needed all them thinners?"
Jasper sensed the situation,
Fraught with fearful implication,
Then as each ominous omen clicked
He heard John's dreaded words "You're nicked!"

So, just as Fate had had in store,
Jasper now faced a Court of Law,
Before His Honour Archie Browne,
The most hard-headed judge in town.
Incensed that he was being fitted
For a crime he'd not committed.
Jasper didn't have a prayer,
Not with "them thinners" everywhere.

But his fate was sealed beyond a doubt
When the record of his claims came out.
Hearing evidence so substantial,
Albeit mainly circumstantial,
The jury had no other choice
But to return with single voice
A guilty verdict, and so the judge
In passing sentence free of fudge

Spoke of Jasper's arsons past,
And hoped that this would be his last;
And since he gave him fifteen years
That's less naive than first appears.
Imprisoned now in the County jail
He tastes each day Fate's bitter pill.
Despite his being not to blame
He'd lost his house but could not claim,

And, shattering his equilibrium,
He'd only just renewed the premium.
In tears he agonizes nightly
That he was wrongly wronged. Nay, rightly!
For when guilty he was quite content
For the world to deem him innocent.
Espousing values so perverse
Entails accepting the reverse.

So, gentle readers, shed no tears
O'er his imprisonment for years.

What's more, up there, our Percy waits
Beside St Peter's pearly gates,
Bedecked in his celestial raiment
And bent upon exacting payment.
With blow-torch lit and in his hand
His course of action's neatly planned;
When it's time for Jasper Sly to pass
He's going to singe *his* flaming arse!

* * *

THE QUINQUENNIAL CONVENTION

Amos Lovejoy, undertaker, looked at his reflection in the bedroom wardrobe mirror with quiet satisfaction. His dress suit, though old, had brushed up well. His trousers were tighter around the waist than they had been a year ago, but still comfortable. His skill in fixing his bow-tie was undiminished. His shirt cuffs protruded from the sleeves of his dinner jacket just enough to show off his gold cuff-links with the tiny diamond inserts. He looked at his reflection, turning sideways, first left then right, and was pleased with the result.

"How do I look, dear?" he asked Arabella, his wife. It was a rhetorical question but he was pleased with her confirmation just the same.

"You look very smart indeed, dear," she replied, putting down her sherry glass. "I'm sure they'll be very impressed."

The day was no ordinary day for Lovejoy. It was the day of the Undertakers Quinquennial Convention, when each master-undertaker throughout the county exhibited his finest casket in a bid to have it adjudged supreme. This accolade carried with it two benefits. First the winner was awarded the Medallion d'Honneur which only he could portray on his letterheads and correspondence. Secondly he was automatically appointed Master of the Honourable Guild of Undertakers for the next five years, a position coveted by all the undertakers, but none more so than Lovejoy and his bitterest rival, both socially and professionally, Bertram Brasted. It is sad but necessary to relate that the men's rivalry was shared by their wives, for Arabella Lovejoy and Evangelina Brasted had been at each other's throats ever since Evangelina had been heard to describe Arabella, with a certain degree of truth, as an alcoholic sponge. Their feminine rivalry was fuelled also by their individual wish to be appointed the next Chairwoman of the W.I.

The coffin that Lovejoy was exhibiting was the Mk IV version of the 'Peace-of-Mind'® casket which had been born out of the funeral of the late Albert Gold. It now lay in the Chapel of Rest in his funeral parlour awaiting conveyance to the Imperial Hotel in Nutchester where, in the ante-room of the ballroom, the exhibits would be judged by the Mayoress, by the Bishop of Nutchester, the Rt. Rev. Dr Robert Swineforth, and by Lady Doryce Hamilton-Sprong, the Chairwoman of the Women's Institute. It had been Lovejoy's intention to transport the casket himself, but he and Arabella, together with the other undertakers and wives, had been invited to attend a reception to be given by the Mayor and Mayoress prior to the Convention's formal commencement. He had therefore given the necessary instructions on this matter to his assistants, Eric Wrigley and Samuel Hedges, upon pain of death. Now he and Arabella, in her best frock and showing signs of a visit or two to the sherry decanter, set off for the reception.

*

Eric and Samuel were in no hurry to please old Lovejoy, so with time at their disposal they sat playing cribbage upon the lid of a coffin in which lay the remains of Billy Watkins aged 92, who awaited burial the next day, and alongside which lay Lovejoy's 'Peace-of-Mind'® casket. Their game eventually over, Eric brought the hearse to the side entrance of the funeral parlour and backed it close against the half-door, on the other side of which stood the counter along which coffins were rolled into the hearse. Having positioned the hearse he called for Sam in the Chapel of Rest to place the coffin onto the rollers so that it could be gently fed into the hearse.

"Which coffin's that, then?" Sam asked.

"The one on the right," Eric answered.

"Right you are then," Sam said, and placed the coffin on *his* right onto the rollers, an error which neither he nor Eric spotted. That manoeuvre completed, both men set off for the Imperial Hotel, unaware that they were now transporting the mortal remains of Billy Watkins aged 92.

By prior arrangement they drove to the trade entrance of the hotel, where half a dozen hotel employees had been deputed to assist the various undertakers as their coffins were offloaded, under the eagle eye of Mr Crackenforth, the Secretary of the Undertakers Guild. With help from two such hotel staff, Eric and Sam carried their casket into the ante-room and laid it carefully upon the stand designated for the Lovejoy exhibit. That job completed, they drove the hearse back to the funeral parlour in Nutcombe.

The Secretary checked his list and satisfied himself that all of the coffin entries were now in place with their lids slightly askew to permit a glimpse of the linings. He closed the ante-room doors and placed a red rope supported by two chromium posts in front of them to rope the room off. He returned to the reception and announced that as the exhibits had all been positioned, the ante-room was now out of bounds until the judging.

The reception was proceeding merrily, Arabella in particular hugely appreciating the bubbly being offered freely by the waiters. Not wishing to offend them she accepted a further glass whenever they passed. Among the invited guests was the vicar of the Parish Church of Nutcombe, the Rev. Claud Higgins, together with his lovely wife, Joyce, the

Bishop's favourite niece. Despite the Secretary's announcement, Lovejoy remained anxious as he had not witnessed the positioning of his exhibition casket. He tried unsuccessfully to drag himself away from the vicar, who was complaining about Eric's casual approach to his vocation, in particular his winking and smiling at the girls as he helped bear coffins into the church. The approach of the Bishop and Lady Doryce now made Lovejoy's escape impossible. He was trapped.

"Ah, Bishop," said the vicar, "allow me to introduce Mr Lovejoy, our local undertaker." The pair shook hands.

"Aren't you the fellow who fits his coffins with a quick release mechanism?" asked the Bishop.

"That is correct, my lord. My entry today features my Mark IV version with a crush-bar mechanism for rapid exit."

"Why the devil do you think it's necessary? You put the dead uns into the coffins, don't you, so you can see whether they are dead or alive. Have you ever come across one still breathing?"

"It is not my decision to make such coffins," answered Lovejoy, "but the customers who demand it. I give them the choice and most choose those with the mechanism. I must say that I can't blame them after poor Albert Gold's funeral. The deceased's loved ones are anxious to avoid any such grievous possibility."

"But you are causing unnecessary worry," interposed the vicar. "You are making people fearful of dying."

"I would have thought the Church does that with its talk of hell and damnation," the undertaker retorted testily.

"My word," said the vicar. "You are sounding just like old Billy Watkins."

"Who the devil is Billy Watkins, Claud?" asked the Bishop.

"He is, or was, one of our oldest inhabitants. Mr Lovejoy and I will see him buried in our churchyard tomorrow. Many's the discussion I've had with him on religion. He is, or was, very critical of the Church and its teachings and dogma. He didn't think much of Church hierarchy and didn't believe in saints and sainthood. I doubt very much whether he even believed in God."

Lady Doryce was aghast. "Am I to understand," she gasped, "that he will be buried in the churchyard tomorrow? How often do you bury a non-believer in the church grounds, may I ask?"

"Just the once, Lady Doris," Joyce answered. "None of them ever needs burying a second time."

"This is not a subject for flippancy, young lady. And if you wouldn't mind, my name is Doryce, D-o-r-y-c-e!"

The Rev. Claud Higgins was keen to assuage her ladyship. "Lady Doryce, I can assure you that Billy Watkins was a very good man, all that a good Christian should be. If his soul is now aloft, as I am confident it is, then I am sure that St Peter will have welcomed him with open arms. I will of course pray for his soul, aloft or below, but I can say with the utmost confidence that I know exactly where Billy Watkins is right now."

The pause in the conversation gave Lovejoy the opportunity to slip away so that he could check that Sam and Eric had carried out his instructions to the letter. He stole silently along the corridor, unhooked the rope in front of the ante-room door and crept to his designated stand. Once there he shrieked with horror as he saw Eric's ghastly mistake. He slid back the lid of the coffin further and blanched even whiter than Billy Watkins' lifeless face as it peered up at him. Panic seized him. He took out his half-hunter and checked the time. There was less than an hour before the judging. Throwing decorum to the wind he rushed to the hotel reception and grabbed the desk telephone. Fortunately for him Eric was still on the premises to answer his urgent call. He barked his instructions, threatening Eric and Samuel with gruesome embalming if they failed to carry them out. Then, sweating profusely, he returned to the reception.

"Oh *there* you are, my dearest," said the gently swaying Arabella by way of a greeting. "You look as if you'd just seen a ghost!"

*

At the funeral parlour Eric put down the phone and turned towards Samuel. "We've dropped a flaming clanger, Sam," he cried. "We've only been 'n gone 'n taken the wrong coffin to the hotel! Old Lovejoy will have our guts for garters if we don't get the right one there in time. He says we've got half an hour, no more."

"We'll never do it," said Sam. "Nutchester's ten miles away, and our hearse wasn't built for speed."

"We've got to," insisted Eric. "You go and get the hearse round to the side while I get on to the police station!"

He phoned the station and spoke to the sergeant. "We must have a police escort in order for us to get to Nutchester as quickly as we can. It's really important, sergeant," he pleaded. "The Mayor and the Bishop will be there, not to mention Lady Doryce, and if Lovejoy's casket is not there in time, the name of Nutcombe will be dragged through the mud. It's likely to have a serious effect on the whole village, including your own standing, your promotion and your pension."

"Well, lad," said the sergeant. "If it's that important I'll do all that I can. PC Banks is in the station. I'll get him to go round to you with the old Wolseley."

With the correct coffin in the hearse and with the police car leading, the group set off at speed for the hotel, headlights flashing and bell ringing. Onlookers were astonished to see the hearse travelling at 60 mph, and rounding corners on two wheels.

"If the bloke's already dead," quipped one, "surely he won't mind waiting a few minutes for his burial!"

"He might want to be both the quick and the dead," responded his friend.

The convoy made the journey to the side entrance of the hotel in twelve minutes, a record unlikely to be bettered. After bringing the hearse to a screeching halt, Eric and Sam, together with help from the hotel staff, unloaded the exhibition casket and carried it, huffing and puffing, along the corridor into the roped-off ante-room, and stood it on end against the wall adjacent to Lovejoy's designated stand. They then set about taking the coffin containing Billy Watkins to the awaiting hearse. Eric grasped one end while Sam grasped the other. They managed to lift it barely an inch from the stand before letting it fall back with a bang. It was far too heavy for the two of them to lift, let alone carry. They looked at each other in dismay.

"We're not going to do it," moaned Sam. "Let's get those hotel blokes back to help us."

"We can't let them see the corpse!"

"Perhaps we should ask old Lovejoy to come and help us then."

"Don't be daft!" said Eric. "We can't go into the reception dressed like this; and if we go up to Lovejoy and call him away, that will raise all sorts of questions. I think it would be better if we did this in two stages. Let's take Billy out of the coffin, set him down somewhere and come back for him after we've loaded his coffin on to the hearse."

Sam nodded his reluctant assent and they lifted Billy up and out. They each placed one of his arms over their shoulders and slowly made their way, dragging the toes of Billy's shoes along the carpeted corridor, looking for a quiet and secluded resting place for poor Billy. Coming to the Daffodil Room they looked inside. It was empty. They saw a comfortable armchair close to a potted palm, and there they deposited him, placing his hands in his lap and crossing one leg over the other to give the scene the casual appearance of a sleeping man. They hastened back to the ante-room, lifted the surplus coffin from the stand and made their way laboriously to the hearse. Having safely deposited it on the rollers inside, they sat on the tail-board exhausted by their efforts.

"I'm knackered," complained Sam. "Can't we have a breather?"

Eric looked at his Ingersoll watch. "Yeah, I reckon we've made good time. Let's stop for a smoke."

*

And so they lit up, their delay allowing the unfolding of two events, the first of which concerned Billy.

Mr and Mrs Fraser, guests at the hotel, walked into the peace and quiet of the Daffodil Room to get away from the undertakers who seemed to be monopolising the bar and other areas. They glanced at Billy as they passed, and didn't like the look of his pallor. They went immediately to the reception desk and reported their findings to the manager. The manager too looked at Billy and called for the hotel doctor. The doctor looked at Billy and said, "He's dead!"

"No, no!" cried the manager. "We can't have a death on the premises! You've no idea of the formalities we have to go through when a guest kicks the bucket in the hotel. The police, the coroner, the next of kin, the insurance company. It will disturb all our operations and be very bad publicity. Can't you just say he's very poorly and put him on an ambulance for the hospital? Then when he gets there they'll report him 'dead on arrival'."

The doctor considered the position, including the way his own quiet life would be disturbed by such a death, and eventually agreed. When the ambulance men arrived he told them that the patient was having difficulty breathing, suggested that they gave him continuous oxygen and urged them to get him to hospital before it was too late.

*

The second event concerned Bertram Brasted who caught sight of Eric and Sam making their way out of the hotel with the coffin. Intrigued, he made his way to the ante-room, unhooked the red rope and entered. There he saw Lovejoy's exhibition casket propped against the wall, and not on its stand. He walked over to it and, against all the rules laid down by the Convention Committee, he examined his competitor's casket thoroughly - the woodwork, the brass fittings and the lining. He was filled with dismay, for despite the extreme faith he had in his own entry, he could see that Lovejoy's surpassed his in every respect. The only chance he, Bertram Brasted, stood of gaining the award was the sabotage of Lovejoy's entry. Physical damage was out of the question, for the culprit would clearly be seen to be one of the exhibitors. Some far more devious action was called for, so he left the ante-room and sought help from the most devious person he knew - his wife, Evangelina.

He returned to the reception and went over to her. He told her exactly what he had found and the damage it would undoubtedly cause to his chances of gaining the Medallion d'Honneur. As Bertram was recounting his tale of woe, Evangelina gazed continuously with bitter animosity at a dazed and almost comatose Arabella as she lay sprawled upon an armchair, and when Bertram had finished, it occurred to Evangelina that the means for both her and her husband to achieve the objects of their desires lay in Arabella's drunken condition.

"Follow me, Bertie!" she commanded, and walked over to the inebriated Mrs Lovejoy. Feigning solicitousness, they raised her from the armchair and escorted her to the ante-room. There, as Arabella finally sank into a sea of alcoholic haze, they placed her upright into the leaning coffin and replaced the lid. They sought the help of three hotel employees and together they placed the casket on Lovejoy's stand, leaving the lid askew the stipulated amount. They then returned to the reception with self-satisfied smirks upon their faces.

*

Having finished their cigarettes and feeling refreshed, Eric and Sam returned to collect Billy Watkins. They made their way to the Daffodil Room only to find that the armchair was amazingly empty.

"Is this the right room?" asked Sam.

"Yes! I remember the palm. Where the devil can he have got to?" They began their search of the lounges and the bar but without success. Sam made his way to go downstairs. "Where are you going?" asked Eric.

"Well," replied Sam, "I thought he might have gone downstairs for a pee." At this moment Mrs Fraser approached them.

"Are you looking for your granddad?" she asked. "I'm sorry to have to tell you that he was taken ill and has been taken to hospital. I do hope he recovers, only he did look very ill."

"We've got to get to the hospital," urged Sam after Mrs Fraser had gone.

"Yes," agreed Eric, "but first we have got to put the right casket on the stand." They went back to the ante-room and saw the casket in its correct place. "Old Lovejoy must have done it while we were outside. OK, now we can set about retrieving Billy Watkins."

The pair rushed back to the hearse and set off for the hospital. Arriving there they parked the hearse in the car park and went inside to the reception desk. "We're enquiring about an old man who has just been brought in," began Eric.

The receptionist looked at him sympathetically and said, "Just wait here and I'll get the doctor to see you." The doctor duly arrived.

"I'm very sorry," he said, "But in spite of all our efforts he passed away peacefully. If it helps, I am sure he felt no pain."

"Can we see him?" asked Eric.

"Yes, certainly, if you'd follow me." He led them to the mortuary holding bay where Billy was lying peacefully on a trolley. "I'll leave you to grieve for a while," the doctor said, and left.

"Right!" said Eric. "Let's get him out of here!" They wheeled the trolley swiftly the way they had come and out of the hospital's main doors. They rushed to the car park to where the hearse stood, and heard the cries of two hospital porters who were making their way towards them, shouting "Hey you! Stop! Come back here!"

Sam went to open the tailgate. "We haven't got time!" cried Eric. "He'll have to sit inside up front with us." They lifted him in and sped away at speed, tyres screeching and making smoke, leaving the empty trolley where it stood.

"BODY SNATCHERS IN NUTCHESTER" read the next day's headline.

*

Back at the hotel the reception came to an end and the assembled guests were ushered into the ante-room. Lovejoy searched for his wife in vain. The judges made their way along the line of caskets, sliding the lids along, examining the joinery, the brass work and the silk and satin linings of each in turn. Lovejoy's was to be the last examined. Bertram Brasted made his way to stand beside him.

"You looking for your wife, Lovejoy?" he asked. "Would you like to know where she is? She's in your casket, the one the judges are approaching now! You'll be the laughing stock of the county when they move that lid aside! You'll never win the Medallion, Lovejoy, nor get the Presidency. Not this year, not ever!"

Lovejoy's world fell apart. No Medallion, no Presidency, just utter humiliation.

The judges approached the final casket and as they did so, Arabella stirred in her drunken stupor. She rolled over onto her side, so activating the patented quick release mechanism. The side of the casket fell down on its hinges and Arabella fell with a thump onto the floor in front of the judges. The vicar rushed forward to help put her on her feet and as he bent forward he sensed the full extent of her alcoholic intake.

"She is dazed by the fall," he chivalrously announced.

Lovejoy seized the moment. "Yes!" he cried. "But better dazed than buried alive, thanks to the Lovejoy patented escape mechanism!"

Believing the event to be part of a cleverly devised publicity stunt, the assembled guests applauded. It goes without saying that the judges declared Lovejoy's casket to be the worthy winner of the Medallion d'Honneur, which led automatically to Lovejoy's appointment of the Presidency. While he achieved his ambition, his wife, Arabella, did not achieve hers, though she did manage to get a very good price for her prolonged stay at the Sunshine Detox Sanitarium.

*　*　*

THE COUNTY BUS STRIKE

Ronald Ross, the boss of the County Branch of the Bus and Coach Drivers Union, led the three man delegation into the Board Room to put forward the Union's ultimatum to Leonard Bradshaw, the Managing Director of the Shire Bus and Coach Company, who was sitting with his two fellow directors.

"Following the breakdown of talks relating to our demand for an across-the-board pay increase," Ronald Ross said, "I now give you the notice required by our Agreement that my members will be withdrawing their labour three weeks from tomorrow unless the Company meets our demand in full."

Leonard Bradshaw raised his eyebrows in surprise. "Three weeks from tomorrow?" he asked. "Are you serious?"

"Perfectly, Mr Bradshaw, unless the Company sees fit to meet our justified demand."

"I think you're making a mistake, Ron, but if that's your decision...." He did not feel the need to finish the sentence.

"It is, Mr Bradshaw. Three weeks from tomorrow," Ron repeated, and having fulfilled his immediate duty he led his delegation back to the works floor.

One of his co-directors looked anxiously at Leonard Bradshaw. "That will be at the start of the schools' half term, Len. We'll need to implement some contingency plans."

"Forget it, Dick," the Managing Director replied. "The union will cave in, you mark my words. There is something that Ronald Ross has surprisingly forgotten. He has just made a grave mistake."

Ronald Ross had indeed made a grave mistake, in fact a very grave mistake indeed, one which would affect both men's lives in a way neither of them suspected.

Although the two men were adversaries business wise, their private and social lives were closely intertwined. At one time they had been great friends. They were local lads who had attended the Nutcombe primary and secondary schools together, where they caught the eye of many a schoolgirl. They each had passed the Scholarship and had gone on to the Nutchester Grammar School, after which their paths diverged. Len went on to Oxford University while Ron took an apprenticeship at the Shire Bus and Coach Company which was run by Len's father. In the year that saw the completion of Ron's apprenticeship Len returned from Oxford and joined the bus company. He was fast-tracked through the training which had taken Ron five years to complete, and was whisked upstairs to work alongside his father. This was the root cause of the rift in Ron's and Len's relationship. Ron had always considered the two were equals and sensed an injustice which had promoted Len merely by accident of birth. He thought that all accidents led to injuries, in this case his own. His socialist upbringing had instilled in him a hatred of privilege, and he devoted ever more time to the union activities by way of compensation.

However, the relationship took an upward turn two years later when they both married local girls, for Ron's wife, Jane, and Len's wife, Pat, were bosom friends. The two men were thus forced to meet together socially for their wives' sake, and when each of the girls produced an offspring, the foursome was knit together more tightly. For a couple of years the tension was eased, only to be substantially increased when Len, then aged 30, was appointed to the Board of the Company. The war intervened and both men joined the services, Len in the R.A.F. and Ron in the Army, and at the conclusion of the war they re-joined the Company. That same year Len's father died, not yet 60, leaving the controlling interest in the Company to Len, who thereupon became the Managing Director. Ron felt this injury far more than the many others he had conjured up in his mind, and the antagonism he thereafter displayed in his union activities blighted his advancement in the Company.

*

Ron and Jane's daughter, Sophie, was an attractive, high-spirited girl, the image of her mother who, in her early forties, still caught the eye of many a passing male.

Len's wife, Pat, was equally young and attractive, and their son, Michael, was a catch for any perceptive young girl.

As happens in life, Sophie and Michael, who had known each other all their lives, now decided they would marry. They received the blessing of their parents, and the date for the wedding was fixed. Jane and Pat entered enthusiastically into the wedding arrangements, the dresses, the guest-lists, the reception, the flower arrangements and the many other details that necessarily attend the most important day of any girl's life. Everything was proceeding smoothly; that is until Ron made his very grave mistake, for he had called the bus strike for the very same day as the wedding! How he could have overlooked such a fact was beyond Jane's comprehension, for the wedding was uppermost in her mind throughout every single day.

As Ron entered his house that evening, even before he had taken off his jacket, Jane lambasted him.

"What on earth were you thinking? You're Union mad! There's only one union you should have in your mind and that's Sophie's union to Michael. Fancy calling a strike for their wedding day! Or did that small matter not enter your mind? How are the guests supposed to get to Nutcombe with a county-wide bus strike in force? You really astonish me! You carry on about industrial relations, but what about your blood relations? Don't you care about them? When you are escorting Sophie down the aisle, will you be thinking of your rank and file? And when you're in the vestry signing the Register, will your mind be focussing on a picket line somewhere? You've got to get your priorities right! Get on the phone straight away and tell your committee that you're calling the strike off!"

Ron was taken aback, both by the ferocity of the Managing Director intensified.

Jane's outburst and by the fact that until that moment he had overlooked the date of his daughter's wedding. Len's earlier words now came back to him: "Three weeks from tomorrow?" he had said. "Are you serious? I think you're making a mistake, Ron, but if that's your decision...." He now realised that Len had been fully aware of the mistake he was making and had willingly let him mire himself in trouble. His dislike of

"I'm so sorry, Jane," he said. "I can't forgive myself that I missed that connection. You're right. What was I thinking?"

"It's no good just being sorry. Get on the phone now and call off the strike!"

His mind in turmoil, he sheepishly faced his wife.

"I can't do that, Jane. I'd lose face. Caving in now to that Company Board would be a disgrace and a betrayal. I'd be branded a traitor, a turncoat, a fraud."

"Brilliant! So what do you intend to do? If this strike spoils our daughter's wedding don't expect things to remain the same. I doubt if Sophie would want to speak to you ever again."

The recriminations went on into the night.

*

Things were not that much better at Len's house.

"Why didn't you warn Ron about the date?" Pat asked, but Len chose not to tell her it would not have been in the Company's interest to do so. At the very moment Ron had delivered his ultimatum that morning, he had seen Ron's mistake and how he could capitalise upon it. He knew that Jane would try to talk Ron into calling off the strike, and if and when that happened, as he was sure that it would, the Union's case would crumble into dust.

"It didn't occur to me, dear. I wish it had," he lied.

"Well, it's certainly going to threaten the wedding plans, and to our personal detriment. You must settle this dispute with the Union. Have a private word with Ron and sort out a solution."

Len put in a good pretence of being perturbed. "I don't honestly see what I can do, Pat. It was a Union decision, so the ball's in their court."

"But it will affect us personally," Pat insisted. "Imagine the day: The local press will be in attendance at the wedding taking photographs, while the whole county is inconvenienced by the bus strike. The irony will not be lost upon the press. The two men responsible for all the chaos, you and Ron, now linked by marriage, will be depicted drinking champagne and enjoying yourselves while the general public struggle to get around. We will become a laughing-stock, and that I will not have! I don't care what it takes but you two men have got to sort it out - and quickly!"

Over the next two days the battle raged on in both houses, with Pat lashing Len and Jane bashing Ron. But the two men were intent upon settling a score which had now grown into a crisis.

*

The following day was market day so Jane and Pat, following their normal routine, caught the bus into Nutchester, an essentially Regency town with remnants of its mediaeval past visible in its many alleyways. The centre is Market Square, cobbled areas around which are the principle buildings of a county town – the County Hall, the Public Library, the County Court, the Magistrates Court and the Imperial Hotel.

In the centre of the square stands the old Butter Market building, around which on market days the many stalls are arranged. In one corner of the square stands the war memorial, a bronze figure of Nike, the winged victory, bearing a wreath in one hand and a sword in the other. It sits on a square plinth bearing the names of the 2,498 Nutchester men who fell in the First World War and the names of the 1,128 men and women who were killed in the Second.

Jane and Pat alighted from the bus and made their way along the stalls, buying the fresh fruit and vegetables they needed. When their shopping was ended, Pat said, "I've got to go to the Library to change my books and pick up a couple of others. Why don't you go to Sally's Tea Rooms and bag a table, and I'll join you there in ten or fifteen minutes."

When she returned far later, Jane asked, "What on earth kept you? I've been here nearly half an hour."

Pat sat down, smiled, opened her carrier bag and took out a book. "Do you remember Miss Partridge, our English teacher, giving us a talk about Greek Literature? She said that there were many Greek histories and tragedies in the school library but none of the comedies or satyr plays because they tended to be lewd and not fit for young ladies. Well, I was browsing the shelves and I came across one of them."

She handed the book to Jane who looked at the cover and said, "That's not a book one often sees, Four Plays by Aristophanes."

Pat nodded and smiled in appreciation of her friend's witticism, then went on, "I sat down by a table and skimmed through it to see what naughty bits Miss Partridge wanted to spare us from, and read a page or two of one of the plays, Lysistrata. It was written during the Peloponnesian War between Athens and Sparta, and the heroine, Lysistrata, had hit upon a plan to bring the war to an end. She told the women of Greece they should withhold their sexual favours from their husbands until they saw sense and sued for peace. Well, the Greek wives agreed with the plan, and as one of them said, 'if you can't knock sense into your husband's head, try somewhere lower down instead'."

"And the point is?" asked Jane.

"Well, think about it! Have we been able to knock sense into our husbands' heads? We've nagged them skinny. We've delivered curtain-lectures 'til we're blue in the face, and for what? Nothing! They will not listen to anything we say, but if we deprive them of sex I think that may concentrate their minds, don't you? Alone in the spare bedroom, they'll have all the time in the world to think."

"You mean ostracise them?"

"No, no, no. Quite the reverse. We will still be kind and wifely towards them. We will take care to look attractive so that they can see what they are missing, we'll dress so as to highlight our feminine curves, we'll be subtly perfumed but not too much, in fact do all the things we would do if we were out to catch a beau, but strictly no sex. We'll put an imaginary label around our necks – 'Do not touch these goods until the strike is called off!' What do you think?"

Jane laughed. "Brilliant!" she said. "When do we start?"

On the bus on the way back home, Pat said, "I suppose Sophie has told you that she and Michael are sending their fathers to Coventry until the strike is called off. That will help our campaign as well. Do you think you will miss the sex?"

"Not really," Jane replied. "Sometimes it's nice to know you can safely get into bed just to sleep." Then she started to laugh as a memory from the past surfaced. "I've just remembered an incident when Ron and I were on holiday in digs in Skegness. We were lying in bed when we heard the woman in the next room cry out, 'Will you please stop prodding me in the back with that thing!'"

*

The husbands were told of their banishment to the spare bedroom when they arrived home, and were far from overjoyed at the news.

"That's crazy!" said Ron. "How will creating a domestic problem help to solve an industrial one?"

"The domestic problem, as you call it," replied Jane, "was created by you when you forgot the date of your daughter's wedding, so don't try to make out it's my doing. Having upset two families with your thoughtlessness you obviously think that things will carry on as usual. Well, it's time you learnt differently. Your daughter will not talk to you, and you will find your pyjamas laid out in the spare room. You should think yourself lucky it's only temporary. You've only got to call off the strike before the wedding for things to return to normal. And that is all I have got to say on the subject so don't waste your time thinking you can change my mind!"

*

In the Bradshaw household the atmosphere was similarly charged.

"But why me?" cried Len. "I didn't call the strike; the Union did, so why should I suffer?"
"It takes two parties to resolve a dispute, Len, the Company being one of them. You know that the Union always has the power to call a strike, yet you forced them into a corner until they had no other choice. On top of that you failed to warn Ron of his choice of date. Ron can't solve this dispute on his own except by caving in, which he will never do. The pair of you must resolve the issue, and until then your pyjamas stay in the guestroom. Oh, and by the way, Michael has decided not to speak to you till then."

*

The next morning as Sophie sat at the breakfast table Jane came down still wearing her negligee. "That's not like you to come down scantily dressed, Mum," Sophie remarked.
"Oh, I haven't yet decided what to wear today, that's all."
"Well, it looks very sexy, I must say."
Ron appeared. "Morning, darling. Morning Sophie," he said.

Sophie turned to her mother. "Mum, as I am not talking to Dad, will you please tell him that I bid 'good morning' to him too."

"Sophie says …," began Jane.

"I heard," growled Ron.

"And, Mum," Sophie went on, "I was wondering if Dad agrees with me that your negligee looks sexy, but as I'm not speaking to him could you please ask him for me?"

"Sophie asks…," began Jane.

"This is bloody ridiculous!" snarled Ron, and stormed out of the house without eating his cornflakes.

*

In the Bradshaw household Len came down to breakfast grumpy and sulking.

"Morning," he growled.

"Morning, dear," responded Pat, but Michael ignored him. Instead he turned to his mother and exclaimed, "Gosh! Ma, that perfume you've got on is gorgeous. Is it new?"

"No, Michael," she replied. "It's something your father bought me on our honeymoon in France." Then turning to her husband, she asked, "Do you remember, dear?"

"Hmmrph!" he grunted.

"I have kept it as a souvenir 'til now, but I think it would be a shame not to use it. What do you think, dear?"

"Hmmrph!" came the reply.

"Ma," said Michael, "As I'm not talking to Dad, will you please ask him from me why he is sleeping in the guestroom?"

"Certainly, dear. Leonard, Michael wants to know why you are sleeping in the guestroom."

"Hmmrph!" came the reply again.

"Ma," asked Michael, "is this house haunted?"

"What on earth makes you ask that?"

"Well, last night I could have sworn I heard footsteps along the landing and some quiet tapping on one of the bedroom doors. Didn't you hear it?"

"No, dear, I didn't. Did you, Leonard?"

"This is bloody ridiculous!" snarled Len, and stormed out of the house without eating his Shredded Wheat.

*

During the day the two men's anger abated and they each went home bearing a gift of a dozen red roses. The wives each accepted the roses with a "Thank you, darling," but neither offered up their lips to be kissed. For more than a week the charade continued, with the wives standing firm against the onslaught of gifts, and the persistent billing and cooing. Sleeping alone and feeling frustrated, the men increasingly faced the reality of their situation, yet neither one wished to be the first to crack.

With a week to go before the wedding, Len called in one of his fellow directors. "It's clear that the Union is not going to cave in, Dick, so we'd better put some contingency plans in place."

"It's too late for that, Len. We should have done that two weeks ago, but you were so certain."

"So what's the likely financial damage if we have no buses on the road for a while?"

"It's not just financial, Len, and it's not just the buses. We've got the Women's Institute booked for a three-day excursion to the Dales and five day-trips by various schools in the coming week. If we have to call in a competitor from another county to help us out we may have lost the business for the future. Not only that, in ten days' time we've got the French delegation coming over on the proposed twinning visit, and the Mayor and Council have booked a coach to show them around the county. There's no way we could ask a competitor to help us out with that."

In the minutes that that conversation took, Len aged years. He buried his head in his hands and realized that Ron was not the only one who had made a grave mistake that day. He reviewed his options both domestic and commercial and knew he had no alternative but to give in.

"I want you to have a quiet word with Ron Ross, Dick," he said at last, "and tell him that I'll meet him in the back parlour of the Red Lion in half an hour's time."

*

The two men were the only ones in the parlour and faced each other across a round pub table. Len was the first to speak.

"Look, Ron. Let's face facts. This strike was called by you and can only be called off by you. The last offer I made was fair, and you know it. Times aren't good and the Company just cannot afford the claim you put in for. This strike is damaging for all of us and must be called off. I can't do it but your Union can. That's where the onus lies."

Ron let his distaste show. "When Dick asked me to meet you here I thought it was to have some meaningful discussion, but I see all you want to do is repeat your familiar twaddle. I notice that the not-so-good times didn't seem to affect the directors bonus-wise. If you've got nothing constructive to offer, Len, I'll get back to work."

He stood up to go. "Ron, Ron," sighed Len almost in anguish, knowing he was in danger of worsening the situation. "Let's forget all the Union/Company crap. That should be the least of our worries. Dire though that situation is, it's nothing compared to what we are having to endure at home. Together we have loused things up twenty-four carat. If the strike ruins our kids' wedding they'll stop speaking to us for good and we may never again see the inside of our wives' bedroom. I don't know about you, but this celibate state is driving me nuts. I've had no nooky for more than two weeks now, and all because of some Ancient Greek!"

"Tell me something I don't know," cried Ron. "I, too, live in a nooky-free zone, and as I lie in bed trying to force myself not to picture Jane on the other side of the wall, I could weep. Physiologically my mounting testosterone level is playing havoc with my libido. I can't stand it any longer. I love her so much that I don't know what I miss most about her."

"I miss her eyes!"

"... Her sighs!"

" ... Her thighs!"

" ... That prize!"

"Why on earth are we torturing ourselves like this," cried Len, "when we both know that back there at home they are just waiting for us to tell them that the strike's been aborted. Then we will have kisses galore. Look, it's clear that neither you nor I will budge, so let's settle this dispute in such a way that we each can claim a victory. You accept the compromise offer I made last and I'll agree to a vacuous productivity clause about works bonuses."

"No!" replied Ron. "Not a vacuous clause, but one with teeth. Otherwise, no deal."

"OK!" said Len. "You drive a hard bargain, Ron. I don't want a tough cookie like you fronting the workforce anymore, so why don't you join us on the Board? You'd make a bloody good Director of Personnel"

*

The reporters from the Nutchester Chronicle were invited into the Boardroom to hear the news of the end of the strike threat. Len and Ron stood side by side inwardly beaming while trying to look statesmanlike. Len spoke for both of them. "Uppermost in our minds throughout this dispute has been our concern for the travelling public. We have put aside all personal considerations and have selflessly sought a just and honorable solution. It is therefore satisfying to all sides that all our problems have been put to bed."

The next day Jane and Pat met for coffee in Sally's Tea Rooms each eager to hear the other's news. "Did you …er…?" asked Jane.

"Yes, we did," Pat answered, "and very nice it was, too. How about you?"

"Yes, we did as well. And do you know, Ron said 'thank you' afterwards."

The wedding at St Barnabas Parish Church, conducted by the Rev. Claud Higgins, was a joyful occasion, the bride and groom kissing their parents enthusiastically. At the reception, the vicar approached the foursome with a smile upon his face.

"Delightful," he said, "truly delightful to see the parents so closely knit. Oh, by the way, congratulations on your new appointment Mr Ross. As I was saying, I conduct many marriage ceremonies knowing that the happy couple's parents will hardly ever see each other again. Do you know, I blame the English language. We do not have a word to describe that relationship. As we haven't got such a word they have to describe themselves as 'happy-couple's parents-in-law' which is hardly conducive to a close relationship, is it? However, the Greeks do have such a word."

"Oh! God!" Ron groaned under his breath. "The bloody Greeks again!"

"Yes," continued the vicar, spreading his arms towards the foursome, "You are *sympetheroi*!"

"Oh! Bully!" Len whispered.

From the photographs which appeared in the Nutchester Chronicle, many readers commented upon the fact that the happy couple's mothers, the *sympetheres*, looked radiant, dressed in the most exquisite style and each wearing an enigmatic smile.

Thus, with feminine power asserted, the county bus-strike was averted, and as the chastened men assumed, normal service was resumed.

* * *

[Editor's note: This tale is based largely upon the written testimony of two ladies who expressed the wish to remain anonymous.]

COWBOYS

Pamela Palmer was a plump, cheerful, happy-go-lucky lady. Nothing upset her. When Labour won the 1945 election, and her friends urged her to join them in emigrating, she smiled and said it could probably turn out well enough. And when her gooseberry jam failed even to receive a commendation at the W.I. Garden Party she smiled and congratulated the winner. Even when her husband lost the race to beat the express train at the level crossing she allowed herself just one tear at his funeral – though she did miss the Humber Snipe that he was driving at the time. Nothing, it seems, could faze her. She was resilience and fortitude personified. She lived in one of six houses which had been built in the Walled Garden the squire had been forced to sell to meet some of his debts. Her house had not been decorated since before the war and now she thought it was time for a complete refurbishment. To this end she had sought estimates from three contractors to carry out a variety of work and had unwisely chosen the cheapest, that from Messrs Grout & Plaster – 'all work guaranteed, unsolicited testimonials available upon request'. There were no testimonials, of course. Fred Grout and Bert Plaster had taken the words from the literature of their competitors when they had set up their two-man business the previous year.

They had been at Mrs Palmer's house just two days, which was enough time to reduce her cheerful demeanour to that of a nervous wreck. Fred Grout patted her shoulder consolingly as she sat on the dwarf wall in front of her house, sobbing fit to break, with his arm resting upon her shoulders in a vain attempt to comfort her. He finished what he had to say then suddenly stood up and started to walk quickly away. As he did so, Mrs Palmer rose, picked up the nearest object to hand and threw it deliberately and forcefully at his retreating figure. It caught him square on the back of his head and he fell to the ground unconscious in full view of the horrified neighbours.

*

Peter Penny cycled back to Nutcombe, returning from a night spent with Milly, his Felsham wife. As was his custom, he rested his bike against his cottage porch and went inside to the warmth and the smell of coffee and newly baked bread. Peggy, his Nutcombe wife, stepped forward to kiss him.

"Morning, Pet," she greeted him. "And how is Milly?"

"She's grand, Peggy, and sends her love. She's due in six or seven weeks' time."

"That's lovely. I think I'll pop over later and see if she wants a hand."

"She'd love that, pet."

"Now, did she give you your breakfast before you left? No? Right, come back here after you've got the brazier started in the forge and I'll have your breakfast on the table for you when you get back."

When Peter returned he sat down to his usual plate piled high with eggs, ham and sautéed potatoes. Peggy sat at the table opposite him.

"Pamela was asking for you yesterday evening," she said.

"Pamela? Who's Pamela?"

"Pamela Palmer. She lives up in the Walled Garden. You know, the one whose husband got killed at the level crossing a couple of years back"

"Oh her. So what did she want?"

"She didn't say, but she said it was important. I told her you'd probably be in the Red Lion this lunch time and could possibly see her then."

"I'll see her there then," Peter said, "though Lord knows what she could want with me."

"Well," Peggy said, "I don't think she'll be wanting to be your next wife. She'll be drawing a pension in a year or two's time, and I know for a fact, Peter Penny, that you prefer them a bit younger than that. Not that she'd have you, of course."

That lunch-time Peter sat in the Red Lion, his pint of ale in front of him, when Mrs Palmer approached.

"Mr Penny," she said, "it's so good of you to let me see you."

"Sit yourself down, Mrs Palmer, and let me know how I can help you."

"Well, it's a long story, but a week or so ago I was seen by that nice PC Banks, and taken to the police station. There I was interviewed by Inspector Groves and charged with common assault. Then I received a summons to appear at the Magistrates Court in Nutchester. I knew I needed a solicitor so I went to Flint, Flint and Flint and saw the middle one, but he said that he was representing Fred Grout, the man I assaulted. So I didn't know what to do."

"Did you try Warrenders? They're a good firm."

"I couldn't afford their prices, Mr Penny, and anyway, knowing about your reputation with the Law, I would much prefer it if you were to agree to represent me."

Peter's chest filled with pride. He took out his note book and licked the end of his pencil. "Right, Mrs Palmer, tell me everything, right from the beginning." As she detailed all the problems she had had with the workmen he scribbled furiously to record her very words. At the end of twenty minutes he turned to her and said, "I must tell you, Mrs Palmer that this is going to be a hard case to win. You cannot deny that you deliberately assaulted Fred Grout since the police have witness statements from your neighbours to that effect. We could plead 'guilty' and rely upon extenuating circumstances but that would still leave you with a criminal record. I'd much prefer to win on a 'not guilty' plea. Leave it with me. I'll get down to the Nutchester Library and see what I can dig up."

*

The day of the hearing arrived and people in the courtroom rose as Montague Middleton, the Stipendiary Magistrate, approached to take his seat on the Bench.

"Ah, Mr Penny," he said, "And how are your…."

"They're all very well, thank you, your honour. There'll be another one in a few weeks' time."

"What!"

"Kiddies, your honour, not wives."

"Thank goodness for that. You had me worried for a while. But we must get on. Clerk!"

The clerk of the court rose and intoned, "Mrs Pamela Palmer, you are charged with common assault in that you aimed a missile at Mr Fred Grout and rendered him unconscious. How do you plead, guilty or not guilty?"

"My client pleads 'not guilty due to provocation'," said Peter firmly.

"Mr Penny," said the magistrate, sighing audibly. "That is not an acceptable plea in this case. Provocation is available only in cases of murder, and even then is not a complete defence. It merely reduces the crime to one of manslaughter."

"With respect, your honour, I find it difficult to understand why the Law recognizes that one can be provoked to kill, but fails to acknowledge *a fortiori* that one can also be provoked to assault. That's Latin, your honour. It means...."

"I know what it means, Mr Penny, but it doesn't alter the fact that provocation is only available in murder cases."

"It seems to me, then, that the Law takes a more lenient view of murder than it does of assault, since if the missile had actually killed Mr Grout and my client had been charged with murder, she would have had an additional line of defence."

"If I may say so, Mr Penny, that is a ridiculous argument since Mr Grout is not dead."

"Attempted murder, then," suggested Peter. "Then my client *could* plead provocation, thus reducing the crime to attempted manslaughter, and since there is no such crime as attempted manslaughter my client would have no case to answer."

"No such crime as attempted manslaughter?"

Mr Middleton leant over and whispered to the Clerk of the Court who began leafing through the heavy tomes on his desk. As he was doing so, Peter continued, "It stands to reason, your honour. If you kill unintentionally, that's manslaughter, but you cannot *attempt* to kill unintentionally. Attempting means trying, and trying implies an intent. *Ergo* attempted manslaughter is impossible, since it amounts to a contradiction in terms."

At this point the Clerk looked up at Mr Middleton and shook his head, signifying that the blacksmith might after all be right. However, the magistrate sought to regain the initiative. "Mr Penny," he said, "I have allowed myself unwittingly to be side-tracked by your specious argument. The defence of provocation is not available in your client's case, and I shall therefore enter a plea of not guilty on your client's behalf. Now we shall proceed. Mr Flint?"

The prosecution rose to present its case. Mr Ephraim Flint briefly outlined the facts of the case then called his first witness, Mr Fred Grout, who detailed the damage which Mrs Palmer had inflicted upon him – recurring headaches, nightmares, loss of sleep, anxiety, inability to concentrate, panic attacks, worry, loss of appetite, in fact everything short of dandruff. When he had finished his fanciful peroration, Peter rose to ask, "May I be permitted to question this witness, your honour?"

"Yes, of course, but before you begin, Mr Penny, since you are a man of plain words, perhaps you can tell the court what exactly the missile was that the prosecution alleges your client threw."

"Certainly, your honour. It was a pound of pork sausages. A pound of Henry Lambton's finest."

"Of course," muttered Mr Middleton. "I wonder why that never occurred to me! Do please carry on."

"Well, Mr Grout," Peter began, "or may I call you Fred? To save the Court's time I will not question the facts as set out by your solicitor. I think he presented them succinctly and accurately, but....."

"Hold it right there, Mr Penny," Mr Middleton intervened. "You are accepting that your client threw the missile, er the sausages, but we have entered a 'not guilty' plea. I do not understand."

"It's a question of *mens rea*, your honour. Your honour may recall when I was before this court...."

"Yes, Mr Penny, I remember it well."

"Well, your honour, my client is relying upon that maxim. She had no intention whatever of inflicting a common assault upon Mr Grout."

"But, my dear chap, she deliberately threw the miss ... the sausages at him!"

"Yes, your honour, but not with the intention of committing mere common assault. She intended to inflict grievous bodily harm!"

"Stop, Mr Penny! I must caution you that you are placing your client in greater peril. Causing grievous bodily harm is a far more serious charge than common assault. You are risking her being charged with that."

"With respect, your honour, my understanding of the law is that once a person has been found not guilty of a charge, the prosecution cannot bring further charges on the same facts without new and compelling evidence."

"That is so, Mr Penny, but your client has still to be found not guilty of the present charge."

"We accept that, your honour, but as I develop my questioning you will see that in no way could any reasonable person have intended to commit a mere assault against the complainant."

"Against my better judgement I will allow you to proceed, but if I find you are wasting the Court's time with a frivolous defence I shall deal with you harshly."

"Thank you, your honour." He turned to face Fred Grout and addressed him as one artisan to another. "As you may know, Fred, I'm a blacksmith, so as far as I'm concerned it goes without saying that you carried out your work for Mrs Palmer with the usual high standards of skill and expertise, like we all do. Am I right?"

"Of course."

"That's with the usual snags and setbacks we all encounter from time to time?"

"You're right there, mate."

"Like that bit of bother when you drove up into the drive, eh?"

Fred Grout smiled. "Yeah, that was a bit awkward, but she went over the top about it."

"In what way?"

"Well, like I said to her, really, Mrs Palmer," I said, "You mustn't take on so. These sorts of mishaps happen to everyone all the time. I told her that the solution is to learn how to bear them, as we professionals have to. Take her car, for instance. We were sorry that we scraped the side of it with our lorry when we backed in. The driver just didn't expect there to be a car on the drive. He apologised, but she complained that she heard him repeatedly using the effing word. But he would never use such terms in front of ladies."

"Apart from the car, was there any other damage?"

"Yeah, a bit, but it wasn't the driver's fault for what happened to her television aerial. After he saw that he was scraping the side of her car he pulled hard over to the left – oh yeah, sorry about her rear bumper; I'm sure the garage will be able to fix it back – as I was saying, he pulled sharply over to the left and his near-side mirror caught the slack in her TV aerial cable. I watched as the aerial came crashing down and I thought, 'allo, someone has made a very shoddy job of fixing that to the chimney otherwise it wouldn't have come crashing down like that'. Now, we can't be blamed for someone else's shoddy workmanship, can we? So I told her it would best if she claimed it on her own insurance. I'm sure she'll recover the cost of all her missing tiles – and, of course, the greenhouse roof as well."

"And what about her cat?"

"Yeah, that was another thing she got cross about. We were burning off the paint from the front room wainscoting when he happened to come too near the blow-torch flame. Persian blue, he was. Lovely cat. Well, although his rear end was badly singed you could tell he was fit and strong by the way he shot out of the front door. Just like a bat from out of hell he was! But I told her she shouldn't worry about it because she'd see his fur was bound to grow back soon – that is, of course, if he was ever found".

"Mrs Palmer must have been getting on your nerves by this time, wasn't she, what with her complaining all the time?"

"You can say that again! Take the pond, for example. That was a rum do. I know we shouldn't have emptied the remainder of our industrial strength cleaner into it, but we weren't to know that she was breeding specimen koi carp in it, were we? I saw that they were all floating upside down, and I asked her if she was sure that that meant they were definitely dead. She said it certainly did and started to cry, so I tried to console her by saying that it only went to show that we never really know what lies ahead of us around the corner. I can't be sure, but I think it was a blessing that it turned the water that much warmer for them as they went. And that water did turn a lovely shade of mid-green. One of Nature's colours that, as I told her, but she didn't seem interested."

"None of us can be expected to cope with what other people do, can we?"

"No, there's no rhyme nor reason to it sometimes. I ask you, you'd think that they would standardise the location of stop-cocks, wouldn't you? They should all be under the sink somewhere so you could get to them quickly. If hers had been there we could have stopped the flow from the bathroom long before it soaked the dining-room ceiling and brought the plaster down. Pity about her table setting. It looked expensive. Royal Worcester, I think it was. Anyway, about the bathroom, we had to use quick-setting cement to set the W.C. in position, but it had set before we had aligned the pan correctly. It was alright when you sat on it. You could still do your business OK, except you'd be sort of 45 degrees askew. The upside was that she now had a little more space in front of the wash basin, and the fact that they didn't quite colour-match wasn't so obvious."

"That must have upset her?"

"Too right. I tried to calm her down. I reminded her that the pills she took earlier certainly made her calmer and suggested she took another couple. Honest, at one time I really thought that she was going to have a seizure when we were using the steam-and-strip machine in her living room. How it came to vaporize her TV screen I'll never know. Nor how that came to blow the fuse in her fridge-freezer. It's a pity we didn't notice that earlier, otherwise we might have been able to save all the contents from defrosting. I told her I supposed it would all have to be thrown away, and to help her out, we took away the pork chops, the kidneys and the sausages, because we were not afraid to risk it, and we would never have come back on her if we got salmonella or anything."

"I can see your point. Was that it?"

"Well, I couldn't help feeling that she wasn't too satisfied with some of our work, so I told her that when we got back to the office I'd rectify her bill downwards so we didn't lose her goodwill. Now I couldn't say fairer than that, could I? 'We'll be off now, Mrs P,' I said. I could see all her neighbours coming out to support her, which I must say I found very heartening. Then I called to Bert to start the engine quickly and strode away fast."

"I can understand you were most anxious to get away, eh?"

"You bet! As I trotted away, Mrs Palmer picked up the pound of frozen sausages which I had dropped in my hurry to depart. I didn't see it but I understand that she took deliberate aim and threw it straight at my head."

"But why were you in such a hurry to get away, Fred?" asked Peter.

"Well, I could hear the fire engines getting nearer, bells clanging, so I thought it best to be somewhere else."

Mr Middleton could take no more.

"Stop!" he cried. "This is quite disgraceful. You have convinced me, Mr Penny. No reasonable person would have been satisfied with causing a mere common assault in those circumstances, and I accept your statement that your client's intentions were centred upon causing grievous bodily harm. Case dismissed. Inspector Groves, if you would be so kind as to see me in my office, I'd be much obliged. And yes, Mr Penny before you ask, costs to the defendant from Court funds."

* * *

JENNIFER GRAYSON

[Editor's note: My grandfather's tales were always humorous, but this one which I found among his papers is quite dark, which is clearly why he never told it to me as a child.]

The Park Lodge area of Nutcombe was referred to by the indigenous population as 'poshland', for the houses there were well beyond their reach, even the cheapest one costing more than £4,000. They were built with the up and coming generation in mind, to a high specification. They were all detached, with one or even two garages. They were centrally heated with modern kitchens, and the more expensive ones were double-glazed. Many of the owners of these properties were newcomers, but Roger and Jennifer Grayson were true Nutcombe folk who had made good, Roger as an accountant and Jennifer as a solicitor. They were in their early thirties with two children, Kate, a girl of four and Joshua, a son just turned one. Before Jennifer left the firm of Warrenders as a junior partner in order to start a family, their combined salaries were well over £6,000, amply sufficient to enable them to move to Park Lodge; and Roger's present salary of £2,800 was more than enough to enable them to live an extremely comfortable and happy life.

Roger was the Deputy Finance Director of Grants of Nutchester and on the morning in question he drove to work in his green coloured Ford Zodiac. Jennifer for her part drove Kate to nursery school in her pink VW Beetle and returned home to care for Joshua. At eleven o'clock her telephone rang.

"Hello, Jenny," said Roger, "There's been a change of plan. Simon is ill and I have got to take his place at the conference in Harrogate. I'll have to leave in a couple of hours' time, so could you please pack a case for me with a change of shirt et cetera for a two or three days' stay and bring them to the office here?"

"Roger, how on earth can I manage that? I've got to pick up Katie at twelve. Can't you catch a later train?"

"No, sorry, darling. I know it's a rush, but please do what you can. I must go now. Sorry. Bye. Love you."

Jennifer put down the phone and thought of how best to sort out the problem. She clearly needed help so she phoned the Police Station and asked to speak to her younger brother, PC John Banks. She explained the problem and sought his advice.

"Leave it with me, Sis," he said. "I'll call round now and pick up Josh, and then I'll collect Katie at twelve and take them both to Mum's. You do what you have to and then pick the kids up on your way back from Nutchester."

Relieved, Jennifer hurriedly packed a case for Roger, and once John had collected Josh she drove to the offices of Grants of Nutchester. She entered the building and went to Reception.

"Will you please let Mr Grayson know that I am here," she said.

The receptionist dialled a number then said, "He's on his way down." However, it was not Roger who appeared but his secretary, a tall, striking brunette.

"I'm sorry," the secretary said, "Mr Grayson is in conference, but I will see that he gets this." She took the case and left, leaving Jennifer flabbergasted. She felt that she had just been dismissed. It had all been so matter-of-fact, with no introductions and no chat. And what sort of look had the secretary given her as she had turned to walk away?

On the drive back to Nutcombe to pick up the children she gradually saw things more rationally. It had been a rush, she thought; she had been anxious, and so, no doubt, had Roger. One couldn't just drop things as one wanted. It was a price one had to pay when one was an executive.

That evening, now settled in her mind and comfortable in her routine, she waited for the phone-call she knew would come.

"Hello, darling," Roger said. "I'm sorry about that awful rush, but it really was panic in the office, having to gen up on Simon's work."

"How are you, darling?" Jennifer asked. "And is your hotel nice?"

"Yes, it's great. It's the Strayview Hotel. As its name says, it overlooks the Stray. It's got quite a large conference suite where all the delegates will be meeting for the next two days."

"Did I pack everything you need?"

"Yes, thank you. You are a smashing wife. I love you."

"I love you, too. The children are missing you. They're both in bed now, of course."

"Ah, bless them! Give them a kiss from Daddy, will you?"

After the phone call had ended Jennifer felt her contented self once more and went to bed in a happy frame of mind. She awoke the next morning and went downstairs. Among the mail on the front-door mat was a letter addressed to Mr & Mrs Grayson in an envelope bearing the Strayview Hotel name and logo. She opened it and read:

Dear Mr & Mrs Grayson,

We are writing to confirm your reservation of a double room for two nights from the 14th inst and trust you will enjoy a very pleasant stay with us.

It was dated two days earlier.

The blow was physical. She felt her heart pounding as she dropped heavily into a chair. Two streams of thought fought for supremacy in her mind. On the one hand she wanted to believe that a genuine mix-up had happened – that the letter was intended for another couple – but on the other hand she knew that there was no mistake. The address was quite specific. It was intended for the couple who had booked a double room at the hotel, one of whom was Roger Grayson. She sat for five or ten minutes as diverse thoughts raced through her mind, and in this time her pulse began to slacken. She was now coldly sure that she was being betrayed, but needed to have it confirmed before she took any action.

She carried on with her normal routine that morning so that the children would not sense the anguish she was suffering, then, having taken Katie to nursery school, she phoned Grants of Nutchester.

"May I speak to Mr Grayson or his secretary, please?" she asked.

"I'm sorry, madam, but they are both away for the rest of the week."

"Oh, that's a pity. Is that for the Harrogate conference then?"

"Yes, that's right."

"I think I know his secretary. Is she the tall brunette?"

"Yes, Helen is rather tall."

"I'll try to catch them next week then. By the way, how is Mr Simon Grant now?"

"He's fine. Why do you ask?"

"I heard he wasn't well yesterday."

"No, he's fine. Would you like me to put you through to him?"

"No, thank you. Bye bye."

She ended the call, picked up the letter from the hotel and dialled their number.

"Will you put me through to Mr and Mrs Grayson, please?"

"They won't be in their room now," the receptionist said. "I saw them go into the Conference Room after breakfast. I don't think I should call them out of there unless it's urgent."

"No, don't bother, as long as they managed to book in together OK. That's all I wanted to know. Bye."

Now her worst suspicions were confirmed. Her marriage was irretrievably damaged and she set about salvaging what she could from the wreckage. She phoned her brother John and told him briefly of her betrayal. He called upon her when he came off duty and together they worked out a plan of action, cold, callous and calculating.

That evening Roger phoned again. "Hello, darling. How are you?"

"A bit tired, what with having to cope with you being away. How was your day?"

"Oh, great. I'm really enjoying it. Is that one of the children I can hear in the background?"

"No, that's John. The children are in bed."

"Of course. Well, give them a big kiss from Daddy, won't you?"

"When will you be back, Roger? Do you know?"

"My train's due into Nutchester at six twenty-eight tomorrow evening. I left the car at the station car park so I should be home just after seven fifteen, I should think. I can't wait to see you again, Jenny. I miss you so much."

"I've got to go now, Roger. Sorry. Bye."

*

Roger's train arrived on time at 6.28 pm and he and Helen, his secretary, strolled into the station concourse arm in arm. Jennifer was there with the children, and when Katie saw her father she ran forward to greet him. Roger, astonished, picked her up and she hugged him. Jennifer wheeled Josh in his pushchair towards Helen and said, "If you want my husband, take him, but you should know that he comes as a job lot with two children. Here they are. Take good care of them. They're lovely children." With that she turned around and left the station.

Roger and Helen stood there, dumbstruck, their mouths opening and closing, fish-like, with no words coming out. It was Helen who broke the silence.

"I don't know what that was all about, Roger, but there's no way I'm getting involved with you and your kids."

"I know, but what are we going to do, Helen?"

"*We? We* are going to do nothing, Roger. This is your problem pure and simple. You sort it out. I'm going home." She turned to go when Roger stopped her.

"Hang on, Helen. I can't be left here with the two children and my case. Help me get along to the car park and I'll drive you home."

With Helen holding Katie's hand and guiding the pushchair, and Roger carrying two suitcases, they made their way to the car park unaware that all their actions had been closely watched by John Banks ever since their arrival. They reached the spot where Roger had parked his Ford, but it was no longer there.

"Bloody hell!" he cried. "It's been pinched!"

That was the final straw for Helen. "Right!" she said. "That's it. I'm off. I'll catch a bus." She picked up her case and strode away, leaving Roger helpless and lost, but then he saw his brother-in-law John approaching.

"John!" he called. "The very man! Somebody's pinched my car!"

"It hasn't been pinched, Roger," John said. "Jenny drove home in it. Come along, I'll drive you back to Nutcombe in the police car. It's over there." He picked up Katie and the suitcase and walked across the car park, Roger striding alongside with Josh.

"I can't understand her, John. She saw me with my secretary and obviously thought that something was going on between us."

When they reached the police car John said, "Put the children in the back. I'll stow the pushchair in the boot." That done he closed the car door so that the children would not hear, and rounded on Roger. "Don't give me any more crap, Roger. We know exactly what has been going on. If it were up to me I'd beat seven different kinds of shit out of you right now, but I promised Jenny I wouldn't touch you. But if you feed me any more bullshit I may forget my promise. Now get in the car with the kids and don't say a word until we get back to Nutcombe!"

They travelled in silence, the children soon falling asleep as the police car sped away from Nutchester. On the outskirts of Nutcombe Roger ventured to say, "You should have turned left there, John."

"I'm not taking you to Park Lodge, Roger," John replied. "Jenny doesn't want to see you. I'm taking you to my house. Now shut up until we get there, and then I'll explain the position to you."

When they arrived at the house John's wife Grace opened the front-door for them. They carried the sleeping children inside and as Roger put them to bed, Katie in a bed and Josh in his cot, John went into the living room and picked up the phone. He dialled Jenny's number, let the phone ring twice then put the phone down. He dialled the number again and let it ring until Jennifer answered it. "We're home, Jenny," he said. "No bother. I'll be in touch."

Roger made his way downstairs completely bewildered by the turn of events. "What's going on, John?" he asked.

"You're staying here with Grace and me for the coming week. Jenny is devastated by your betrayal and doesn't want to see you. She needs time for herself in order to get over it. The children have been told that she will be away for a few days and that they will see her again when she gets back next week. Till then you will have to look after them. You, not Grace. She has the baby to look after. We've brought all the things the children will need, their toys, and their changes of clothing. We've also brought some of your stuff. You'll find it all in the wardrobes and cupboards upstairs. If there's anything we've forgotten just let me know. You're in the spare room, by the way. Here's a schedule Jenny has prepared for you, so there shouldn't a problem."

Roger exploded. "What the hell are you talking about? I can't look after them for a week. I've got a job to go to."

"Yes you can. Jenny phoned your boss late this afternoon and told him you had a family crisis on your hands. He has agreed that you should have time off in order to sort it out."

"But I've got to file a report on the conference!"

"He mentioned that. He said your secretary would be able to fill him in with all the details, though I doubt whether she'll tell him everything that went on, will she? Get wise to yourself, Roger! You're the one who has cocked up your marriage, and Jenny is the one left with the problem of sorting it out, and she's got to do it her way." Roger remained silent, so John continued. "I won't be here all the time. I too have a job to do, so you're on your own. Tomorrow is Saturday. Take the kids to the green or somewhere. Enjoy being with them. Feed the ducks, or whatever you like. Just accept the fact that that's your job for the coming week. On Sunday I'm taking you and the children to my parents for lunch. Jenny won't be there, of course. They know about your shenanigans but won't mention it. Then on Monday onwards, just follow the routine set out in Jenny's schedule. Now I've got to leave you. I'm on duty shortly and have got to get the car back to the station. You've been here often before, so you know where everything is. I'll try not to wake you when I come off my shift."

With that he was gone. Roger immediately picked up the phone and dialed his home. The phone rang and rang but Jennifer did not answer it. He tried again many times that night, with the same result, until he went to bed crying.

*

Lunch on the Sunday at the Bankses was a strained affair. Katie and Josh were delighted to see their grandparents, as they were to see them, but as far as Roger was concerned the air was chilled, politely chilled, but cold nonetheless.

On the Monday and the Tuesday he followed the routine set out for him. Many times he phoned his home without success, and on one occasion thought of contacting his office but decided against it. He could not tell what the office knew of his affair. Had Helen bragged about her conquest? Was he now a figure of fun? Did Simon know? He was furious at the way he was being manipulated by Jennifer and her brother, and on the Tuesday evening he decided enough was enough. He dressed his children in their outdoor clothes, put Josh in his pushchair and set off on the long walk to Park Lodge.

He arrived at the house and tried his key. It did not turn. The lock had been changed. He rang the bell and heard Jennifer's footsteps along the hall. As she opened the door he cried, "Look, children, Mummy's back home!"

So confronted, Jennifer had no choice but to let her family in. "It's time they were in bed," she said. "Have they had their bath?" She took them upstairs and put them together in the guest bed, as Josh's cot was at John's. Having done that she went into her bedroom, picked up the phone and left a message for her brother at the police station.

When she returned to the living room she saw that Roger had settled himself in. "You're not staying," she said.

"John said we were only staying with him till Saturday and then coming back home here. So what difference does two or three days make?"

"He said the children would be seeing me again, not you."

"Oh, come on, Jenny. What's the point of all this? I know I've behaved badly and for that I'm truly sorry. It won't happen again, I promise. I've learnt my lesson. Look, I took Katie to nursery school and picked her up again as you wanted."

"I know. I saw you, both days."

"What! You've been checking up on me? Don't you trust me?" The look Jennifer gave him made him realise the stupidity of that remark. "OK. I'm sorry. That was a daft thing to say. But I mean to say, the things you're putting me through, just because I've slept with another woman. It was a one off. It doesn't mean I don't love you, because I do."

"You don't get it, do you, Roger?"

"Lots of blokes have an affair, but they're not subjected to the humiliation you're putting me through."

"Humiliation? You don't know the meaning of the word. Humiliation is packing a suitcase for your husband and handing it over to the women he is intending to sleep with."

"That's not true, Jenny. I didn't know about going to Harrogate, or that Helen was also going, before I rang you on Wednesday morning."

"Don't lie, Roger!" she screamed. "The arrangement was made the previous day." She went to the desk, took out the hotel's letter and threw it to him. "There's the proof! The mistake you made was giving your home address to the hotel. But you had to do that, didn't you? If the arrangements had been made through the company everyone in the office would have known about you shagging your secretary. And you had to wait until the last minute to let me know, so that I would have no time to ask awkward questions or perhaps suggest that I accompanied you. You're pathetic, Roger!"

He sat there, completely abashed. "So what happens now?" he eventually asked.

"We're through, that's what."

"I don't understand. Wasn't my punishment having to look after the children for a week? If you thought we were through, why didn't you just tell me that at the station instead of all this rigmarole?"

"I needed time to be free to do all the things that were necessary following our break-up."

"Such as what?"

"So many things. You want to know what they were. Right, I'll tell you. First of all I've started divorce proceedings against you, so you will need to find a different solicitor."

"You've done what? Aren't you taking all of this a bit too seriously? Christ, I've only slept with another woman, that's all."

"As I said, Roger, you don't get it, do you? I've also drawn up a new will in which you get nothing. I am severing our joint tenancy, so that this house will be owned by us as tenants in common. The Land Registry and the building society will be notified."

"Hold on, hold on! How are you going to manage all this without me? After what you've just said I'm damned if you'll get another penny out of me."

"I expected that, which is why I have transferred everything that was in our joint account into an individual account in my own name."

"You bitch! That won't get you far."

"I know that too, so I've been to Warrenders and they've agreed to take me back as a junior partner. I'll be starting there once I have been able to make the necessary arrangements about Katie and Josh. So you see, we'll be able to cope without you."

He sat for a while, unable to accept that he was beaten. He changed tack. "What about our children, Jenny? For their sakes, why can't we go on as normal but without the sex? You do what you want to and I'll carry on as usual. Our children need a father, and I've been a good father to them, you can't deny that."

She looked at him with contempt. "You cannot be a good father not loving them."

"I do love them. How can you say that?"

"You phoned from the hotel. 'Give the kiddies a kiss from Daddy', you said, and all the while your tart was in the room with you. Was she smiling as you said it, and did you perhaps join in the smile? It wasn't as if you had temporarily forgotten you were married with children. They were uppermost in your mind, for God's sake! You were talking to me on the phone about them. Any husband and father who loved his family would have felt shame at that moment, and drawn back, but not you! You carried on with your affair, not for just that night, but you repeated it a second time. And why? Because you didn't love them, don't love them, just yourself, and the pity is you just don't get it, even now. You think it is only a matter of sexual infidelity. It isn't. You have shown yourself in your true colours. You're a liar, a deceiver, totally untrustworthy. How can you possibly expect me to have anything more to do with you? I cannot live with you anymore, which is why you must leave."

In his bitterness he cried, "Talking of showing yourself in your true colours, I would never have believed I had married such a vindictive bitch as you. You on your high horse! I suppose it has never occurred to you that you have probably ruined my career at Grant's."

"How on earth could I have done that?"

"By preventing me from going into work, that's how. In my absence that stupid cow could have told the other girls about Harrogate. I'm most probably a laughing-stock right now."

"Just as I have probably been for the last two days. I can imagine Helen's gossip: 'She packed his suitcase and brought it here, and even handed it over to me so that her husband could spend a dirty weekend with me!' You're full of self-pity, Roger, and fail to see that it's all your own doing."

Roger could see that his position was indefensible and that he could never win by argument, so he reasserted his legal position. "You can do what you bloody well like. This is my house and I'm staying here, and there's nothing you can do about it."

"It's true that I can't physically eject you now, but tomorrow I'll seek an injunction or restraining order from the court to get the law on my side."

"They'll never grant it," he scoffed.

"Possibly not. But then the reason for my petition will be in the open and your career at Grant's will certainly then be at issue." She stopped talking to answer a ring at the front door bell. She rose and let John enter the house.

"I've brought your two suitcases, Roger," John said, "the one you took to Harrogate and the one we filled for your stay at my house. You'll be needing both tonight, I think. Jenny will send your other possessions on when you have a forwarding address to send them to."

"Who the hell do you think you're talking to?" demanded Roger. "Get out of my house before I throw you out!"

John smiled. "I know you're stupid, Roger, but even you can't be daft enough to think you can do that. And before I forget, I'd like my door key back. You are no longer welcome at our house."

Roger turned to Jennifer. "Jenny! You're my wife, for God's sake. Help me!"

"Goodbye, Roger," was all she said.

As has often been noted, revenge is best served cold.

* * *

THE NUN'S TALE

It was the week of the Nutt County Show and Trade Fair, and Nutchester was abuzz. The Lord Lieutenant and the County Councillors had decided to re-invigorate the County's commerce, agriculture and industry after the gloom and rationing of the war years by re-instituting the County Show, the official opening of which was scheduled for 11 o'clock the following morning.

The Show Ground was decked with flags and pennants; the parade ring was in pristine condition with tannoys ready and in position. At the far end of the ground there were lines of the latest in motorised farming equipment, dwarfing the stalls at the other end of the ground which had been installed for the influx of livestock. Ash-paled enclosures by the dozen had been set up for countryside crafts and exhibits, many taken up by the good folk of Nutcombe. Peter Penny had a grand display of his functional and decorative wrought-iron work; Ron Baker had several firkins of his locally brewed beers for sampling and purchase, thanks to a license granted with pleasure by the magistrates; and Henry Lambton, master butcher, was exhibiting his two sows and their piglets in the hope and expectation of carrying off the golden rosette.

The Exhibition Hall was similarly busy, with large areas allocated to the many trades and industries finding their feet again after the stagnation of the war years. At one end of the hall was an area showing the funerary skills of the Honourable Guild of Undertakers, hosted by Amos Lovejoy, President; at the other end was a display of babies' clothing hand-crafted by the Little Parsley Ladies' Co-operative; while in the centre stood the stand of Spence & Company of Cranbury, manufacturers of games and toys, in charge of which was the Sales Director, Denis Foster.

Denis Foster had all the assurance of a man for whom nothing ever went wrong. He glided effortlessly through life on a combination of charm and good looks, applied as necessary with an utter lack of scruple. Most women found him irresistible, and most men regarded him as too smooth by half. A few years earlier he had joined the Company as a salesman, and was now its Sales Director, an advancement which followed shortly and unsurprisingly after his marriage to the daughter of the owner, Michael Spence. Mr Spence had consented to his staying at a hotel in Nutchester for the duration of the fair, Denis having insisted that it would be necessary for him to work all hours to ensure the success of their display. He was looking forward to the opportunities that would be offered by a few nights 'off the leash,' as he regarded it.

With him was a colleague, Keith Brooks. On arrival at the Exhibition Hall he asked Keith to take his suitcase to the Imperial Hotel and to tell them that he would check in later. He entered the hall and made his way to the Company's stand, looking about him for likely conquests. His eye was caught by an attractive blonde on the very next stand. By the end of the afternoon the two were in flirtatious conversation, and when the hall closed for the day they left together.

They spent the evening dining and dancing. The girl told him that her name was Astrid, that she was from Holland, and that she was staying in a hostel a mile or so from Nutcombe with some other Dutch girls. After dark he drove her back to the hostel. Following her directions, he parked in a lay-by next to a pair of high iron gates. Astrid explained that the gates were now locked, and they must enter quietly by a side gate.

She took him by the hand and led him through the darkness into the building, up to her room and into her bed.

*

Denis awoke in the morning sunlight. He rose, pulled on his underpants, and went to the window. Opening the curtains, he looked up at the sky and stretched contentedly. Then his glance travelled downwards, and he found himself looking at a walled courtyard, full of people passing to and fro. They were all nuns!

Panic-stricken he shook Astrid rudely awake and she stared up at him in horror.

"Good God! Are you still here?" she cried. "Why didn't you wake me earlier? Now we're for it!" She leapt from the bed and started hurriedly to dress.

"What's going on?" Denis asked. "The place is full of nuns!"

"Of course it is, stupid! It's a convent, Nutcombe Priory."

"A convent? You said it was a hostel!"

"It is. The nuns run a hostel for young catholic ladies from abroad."

"Christ! How am I going to get out?"

"It's too late to sneak out unseen. Nuns will be working in the grounds all day. A man would stick out like a – well, never mind what like. For the time being you'll have to hide. Mother Superior will be on her rounds soon, and if she sees you here . . ."

At that moment there was a knock and the door began to open. Denis frantically flung himself on the floor behind the bed. He heard Astrid say, "Oh, it's you, Hannah. You frightened the life out of me," adding, for Denis's benefit, "It's all right, it's only my friend from next door."

Denis rose and smiled sheepishly at Hannah who appraised him with an amused air.

"You're living dangerously," she said to Astrid. "The Reverend Mother could be here any minute, and it's no use your chap hiding under the bed if he leaves these lying around." She picked up Denis's trousers from the floor, and playfully draped them around her neck. "You'll have to get a move on if you don't want to be in hot water when she gets here." With that, Hannah returned to her own room.

While Astrid frantically finished dressing and tidying the room, Denis started to get into his clothes, only to find that his trousers were missing. Belatedly he realised that they must still have been around Hannah's neck when she left.

"Astrid, for pity's sake, go next door and get my trousers back!"

"There's no time, Denis! Mother Superior will be here any minute. Quick! I can hear footsteps now! Get dressed as far as you can, then hide in the wardrobe while the Mother Superior carries out her inspection. When I get back from breakfast I'll get your trousers back from Hannah, and we'll work out a way to smuggle you out of the building".

Denis had no sooner crammed himself into the wardrobe than the Mother Superior arrived with her entourage. She looked around the room and, satisfied, passed on. Astrid could do nothing but join the crocodile of girls falling in behind the Reverend Mother.

When they had gone, Denis assessed the situation. Luckily the opening of the exhibition was not until eleven o'clock. There was still plenty of time to get there. He would get ready and wait for Astrid to return with his trousers. With any luck she would also have come up with a plan to get him out of the convent unseen, and he could then be on his way with time to spare. He found a razor on the vanity unit, and washed and shaved. Then he put his clothes on, sat on the bed, and waited, feeling peculiarly vulnerable without his trousers.

*

Thirty minutes later, Astrid and Hannah returned, each carrying a bundle.

"Good! Let me have my trousers," said Denis impatiently.

"We haven't got them," replied Astrid.

"What! Why not? Where are they?"

"Sister Agatha has them."

"What!"

"I'm sorry, Denis," said Hannah. "I tried to return your trousers the moment I realised I still had them, but as I was about to do so I was spotted by Mother Superior on her rounds. Caught with your trousers in my hands, I had to make up a story on the spur of the moment, so I told her that I had found them outside the boiler room. She assumed that they must have been left by some workmen, and told me to hand them to Sister Agatha."

"Jesus! Now what do we do?"

"We discussed it at breakfast," said Astrid, "and have come up with a solution. We have been to the store room and have borrowed this nun's habit here. It's the largest we could find. You can put it on and leave the convent dressed as a nun."

"But what about my trousers?" he asked, ungraciously.

"If you don't like our suggestion," retorted Astrid, "you will have to go to Sister Agatha and ask for them back. Now stop arguing and put these on!"

The two girls helped Denis to put on the nun's habit in the right order over his own clothes. When they had finished he looked every inch a nun, albeit a rather large and portly one.

"Hannah and I will go now," said Astrid. "Give us five minutes, then leave. Walk slowly and demurely across the courtyard, head bowed, and along the path to the front gates. Walk slowly over to the lay-by and get in your car. We'll be watching from Hannah's car. We'll follow you to your hotel and sort things out from there."

Denis waited five minutes after the girls had left, then straightened his robes and left the room. Following Astrid's instructions he made his way to the gates and walked through. He could see his own car a few yards down the road and with a sigh of relief he turned towards it. As he did so, a firm hand took hold of his elbow, and a voice said "Now then Sister, where do you think you are going?"

He turned to face his captor, and found a nun gazing on him benignly. "This is the way, Sister," she said, and drew him towards the convent minibus and up the step to a seat inside. He sat and looked morosely out of the window at Astrid and Hannah who stood there open-mouthed. He realised he was still trapped among the nuns, but now in a mobile prison, destination unknown.

When the bus was under way, Sister Agatha distributed collecting tins and issued instructions. He found that they were going to solicit funds on the streets of Nutchester, and was cheered somewhat to learn that at least he was heading in the right direction. In the town the minibus stopped at various points to allow the nuns to alight singly or in groups of two or three. He fingered the beads around his neck nervously and prayed that he would be let off on his own. His prayer was answered, and he found himself alone on a busy shopping street.

At last he was free from the nuns. True he was still wearing a nun's habit, but he had his own clothes on underneath, except for trousers. Were it not for that lack, he could doff the habit and take a taxi to the exhibition hall. He started to walk, looking for a tailor's. As he went, passers-by put coins in his collecting tin. He could not refuse them without attracting attention, so he accepted the donations with a grateful smile. Eventually he spotted a gents' outfitters with trousers in the window, and entered hopefully.

The shop assistant was unaccustomed to serving any female customer, let alone a nun. "What can I do for you, Sister?" he asked.

In as high a falsetto as he could trust, Denis replied, "I'd like to see what you have in men's trousers."

The assistant thought, "You shouldn't have become a nun then." Aloud he asked, "What size and colour, Sister?"

"34 waist, 33 inside leg. Navy blue." Seeing the assistant's surprise at his familiarity with masculine measurements, Denis added, "They are for the gardener."

The assistant selected a pair of trousers and laid them on the counter. "Will these do, Sister? Or we have them also with a button fly."

Denis replied. "Oh no, I prefer a zip, it saves so much time,"

Seeing the look on the assistant's face, he hastily added, "I mean, so the gardener says. These will do fine. I'll take them."

He reached instinctively for his wallet in his hip pocket and realised for the first time that it was not only his trousers that were somewhere in the convent, but also his wallet, his money, his driving licence, and his car keys.

Denis had no intention of relinquishing the trousers now that he had them literally in his hand. This was no time for the fainthearted. Looking the assistant straight in the eye, he said firmly, "Put them on our account."

"Do you have an account with us, Sister?"

"The convent does."

The assistant found it hard to believe that a nunnery would have an account with a gentleman's outfitters, but he hesitated to challenge the veracity of a nun. Seeing him waver, Denis added, "If you don't believe me, ask the manager."

Anxious to be relieved of responsibility in the matter, the assistant went into the office at the back of the shop. As soon as he was gone, Denis quickly bundled the trousers up under his voluminous skirt until they were held in place by the girdle around his waist and strode rapidly out of the door.

As he emerged onto the street he was greeted by Sister Agatha's strident voice. "Ah, there you are, Sister. I was wondering where you'd got to. Come along, I have another street for you to do."

"Is there no escape from these pesky nuns?" Denis wondered as he was led rapidly along. At a crossroads they were halted by the traffic until the lights changed. Subtlety was not an option. When they started to cross the road, Denis nimbly turned back and went the other way. Caught up in the flow of pedestrians, Sister Agatha had perforce to continue on her way.

Denis assessed his position. He was once again free of the nuns, and now had a pair of trousers. If he could find somewhere to change into them, he could ditch the nun costume. His only remaining problem would then be recovering his wallet and car keys. Wondering where he might change, he walked along, absent-mindedly fingering the rosary around his neck. He looked up to see the front awning of the Imperial Hotel before him. "Good Lord! These beads really work!" he thought. "I'm home and dry!" With a light heart he entered the hotel and went to the desk.

"Would you tell me the room number of Denis Foster, please?" he asked the clerk.

"I'm sorry Sister, but Mr Foster didn't check in last night and we had to let his room go."

Denis involuntarily uttered an expression which caused the clerk's eyebrows to collide with his hair line. "We kept it as long as we could," said the clerk apologetically, badly shaken. "What with the Fair and everything there's a shortage of available hotel rooms."

"What about his luggage? Is that here?"

"Again, I'm sorry, Sister. We asked the YMCA if they could accommodate Mr Foster should he turn up late and fortunately they said yes, so we sent his suitcase there."

"Christ Almighty!" cried Denis. "Where the hell's this bloody YMCA then?"

"It's by the traffic lights just along the road," replied the clerk, crossing himself furiously, for he was a conscientious Catholic.

Denis walked back into the street cursing his rotten luck, to be so near, yet so far. He should now be changing into his own clothes in the comfort of a hotel room, but instead had acquired the additional problem of errant luggage, requiring yet another mission. Following the hotel clerk's directions, he found the YMCA and approached the desk.

"May I have Mr Foster's case, please?" he asked.

The clerk eyed him suspiciously. Females were not allowed on the premises, but he was not sure whether nuns counted as females or not. "Not unless you have some authority," he said at last.

"I have Mr Foster's authority to collect it," Denis said.

"I can't accept that, Sister. Even if you were Mr Foster himself …" - the clerk smiled at so ridiculous a supposition - "… I'd have to ask you for some form of identification. Now please leave. This is a male establishment and you should not be in here."

"But I must have that suitcase!" Denis cried in exasperation. "And furthermore I'm damned if I'm leaving without it!"

"I think you'd better go before I call the police," said the clerk, pressing a bell concealed under the counter.

Out of the corner of his eye Denis saw other staff advancing. Discretion became the better part of valour. "Good God! Have you no respect for the cloth?" he cried as he fled.

*

Panic was beginning to set in as he ran away down the street. He was still in nun's clothing, and without access to either his money or his luggage. He did have a pair of trousers, but nowhere to change into them. He looked at his watch. Ten forty! He had only twenty minutes to rid himself of the nun's habit and get to the official opening of the Fair by the Mayor.

Turning a corner he saw the canopy above the entrance to the Railway Hotel and made his way swiftly there. If he could change in the hotel, with a bit of luck he could still make it in time. He entered the hotel and followed the signs to the toilets. It was then that the problem struck him with a sickening blow. Which loo should he enter in which to change?

If he entered the ladies' he would leave dressed as a man, while if he wished to come out of the gents', he would have to enter as a nun. He soon concluded that the gents' was the obvious choice, for while he could not be certain who might be around as he left, he could keep watch to ensure the coast was clear before he entered. He counted those going in and coming out, and when he was confident that it was unoccupied he moved towards the door of the men's room.

"Sister!" The hotel porter gripped his arm. "That is the gentlemen's wash-room! Here is the ladies'."

"Let go, you fool!" hissed Denis, struggling to free himself from the man's grip. Salvation was but a door away and no-one was going to stop him now. "Let go, I say!"

"But Sister!" the attendant persisted, tugging him towards the other door.

Denis cracked. He could not face another set-back. "Are you going to let go, or do I have to belt you?"

The porter did not relax his grip, so Denis delivered a right hook to the unfortunate man's stomach, leaving him gasping on the floor.

His were not the only gasps, however. As Denis looked around he saw that he had an astonished and horrified audience, leaving him no other option but to flee. He dashed along the corridor, brushing guests aside, and into the street, where there were taxis standing in a rank. He jumped into the first one and cried, "The Exhibition Hall, and fast!"

*

The taxi made its way to the Fair and drew up at the entrance.

"That'll be seven and six," said the cabbie.

Denis automatically felt for his wallet before remembering that he still had no money, but fumbling to reach his non-existent hip pocket had caused the coins in the collecting tin to rattle.

"Have you got a knife?" he asked.

The cabbie passed him one and watched as Denis cut around the tape securing the lid of the tin and took out the coins to pay him. As Denis entered the hall, the cabbie wrestled with the moral dilemma. He wanted his fare, but doubted that it was right for it to come from a charity collecting tin. On the other hand, it hardly seemed proper to suspect a nun of wrongdoing.

Denis strode thankfully into the hall. He was still in nun's clothing, and still without his money and luggage, but he was now on home territory and could call upon the assistance of Keith. The Mayor had just finished his welcoming address, and exhibitors and buyers were slowly dispersing towards the various stands. Denis looked towards his own display and saw Keith talking to a man whose face Denis could not see. He approached and whispered, "Keith, may I have a word with you, please. It's urgent." At the sound of Denis's voice the stranger turned, and Denis froze as he came face to face with his father-in-law, Michael Spence, the autocratic owner of the Company.

*

Denis and his father-in-law stood looking at each other in mutual astonishment.

"Denis?" said his father-in-law, peering at him incredulously. "Denis? Is that you?"

"Hello, sir," said Denis. "I didn't expect to see you here. Have you come to see how the Exhibition's going?"

His father-in-law refused to be side-stepped. "Denis, what on earth are you doing in that ridiculous costume?"

Denis thought furiously. He couldn't tell the truth – "It all began with my being unfaithful to your daughter, Mr Spence, on my first night away from home." All his native cunning sprang to the fore as he answered, "It's a gimmick, sir." Inventing a story as he spoke, he claimed that the costume was a device to attract buyers' attention, to differentiate their stand from those of their rivals. He had, he said, thought of various ways to exploit the costume in his presentations – "Even a novice will enjoy . . . None of your convent-ional games . . . You'll get into the habit . . Your mother will enjoy our superior games . . ." and so on.

Michael Spence was not wholly convinced of either the effectiveness or the propriety of this novel approach, but as it was too late to alter it, he held his peace and moved away to inspect the other stands.

*

Denis cursed his luck as he took his place on the stand. Because of his father-in-law's unexpected arrival, he was now committed to staying in the nun's habit all day. He was still separated from his wallet and his luggage, but these problems, he thought, he could soon delegate.

To his surprise, his extemporised sales gimmick, with which he was now compelled to persist, did in fact attract favourable attention, and he was kept busy delivering his pun-laden presentation, but in due course there was a lull, and he buttonholed his assistant.

"Keith, I want you to book me a suite at any hotel in town other than the Imperial or the Railway, collect my luggage from the YMCA and take it to that hotel."

He gave him a note of authorisation for the YMCA, and impressed upon him that the hotel was to be instructed to retain the room until he checked in, however late.

That left only the recovery of his money and car keys, and he expected Astrid to help him to accomplish that. She had been taken aback to see him enter the exhibition hall still dressed as a nun, and had observed incredulously as he performed his presentations in that garb. Denis intended to speak to her as soon as the exhibition closed for the day, and get her help in retrieving his trousers, or at least the wallet and car keys from them.

*

As Michael Spence toured the exhibition hall examining his rivals' products, he gave a lot of thought to his son-in-law. He had never really taken to Denis, but his daughter Judy doted upon him, and so for her sake he had suppressed his doubts and given the lad rapid advancement. The previous evening Judy had told her parents that she was pregnant, and it was in his mind to take the opportunity to retire and hand the reins over to Denis. He had come to Nutchester to see Denis in action one more time before making a final decision and, if satisfied, to break the good news to him. His initial reaction on seeing Denis in nun's attire, and hearing his scheme to base his presentation upon it, was to abandon all thought of giving him control of the company. As the day went on though, and he saw the favourable attention his stand was receiving from the buyers and the media, he warmed towards his son-in-law.

Towards the end of the afternoon he approached Denis and with one arm around his shoulders drew him to a quiet section of the stand.

"Now, Denis, you and I must have a chat about the future. Let's have dinner together at the Imperial and we can talk. Shall we say eight o'clock?"

"Yes, of course, sir," answered Denis.

"You'd better drop this 'sir' business and call me Michael from now on."

Denis was astonished, since it had been Mr Spence himself who had insisted on a formal mode of address from the very beginning, and he began to sense the plans which his father-in-law wished to discuss.

"Did you phone Judy last night?" Mr Spence continued, for Judy had told him not to tell Denis her good news before she did.

"No, I didn't get a chance, Michael. As you could see, I've been too busy here today. I'll phone her tonight."

"Best leave it until after we have had our chat," advised Mr Spence, "then you'll have some news for her. See you this evening then, Denis, about eight."

*

When Mr Spence left, Denis smiled in anticipation. If he had read the signs correctly, the old boy was going to retire and give him control of the company. As he stood congratulating himself, Keith returned and told him that he had booked him in at the Belvedere Hotel and had transferred his luggage there from the YMCA. Denis felt a weight lift from his shoulders. After the alarums and excursions of the morning, things were returning to normal. He had only to recover his wallet and all would be well again, and for that he needed Astrid's help. As soon as the Exhibition was over for the day he approached her.

"Astrid, will you help me over one last remaining obstacle. Somehow or other I've got to get my trousers back tonight. It's not just the trousers, but the things in my wallet and my car keys. It's a quarter to six now and I have to meet my father-in-law at eight. How can I retrieve them?"

Astrid thought hard then said, "I think I've got it. Keep the nun's habit on, though put a spare pair of trousers on underneath if you haven't already done so. We'll take a taxi back to the convent right now. By the time we arrive, all the nuns will be at vespers so we will have no difficulty in just walking into Mother

Superior's office and taking them, because the doors are never locked. Then we'll go to my room and you can change out of the nun's costume and back into your own trousers. I'll replace the habit while you walk back to your car in the lay-by, and so back to town. How's that?"

"That sounds fine to me, Astrid. You really are a treasure."

They made their way outside and quickly found a taxi to take them to the convent. On the way, Denis said, "Astrid, can I make a suggestion? Instead of my returning to Nutchester on my own, why don't you come with me? The appointment I have with my father-in-law should be over by ten or thereabouts. I've booked a suite at the Belvedere and am here for the weekend, so why not stay so that we can carry on where we left off?"

She looked at him fondly. "I'd like that very much, Denis. I will need to pack some things, though, so when I have shown you where Mother Superior's office is, I'll dash back to my room and get my things together. You make your way back to my room and we'll leave together."

Arriving at the convent Astrid peeked into the Chapel to check that the nuns were at vespers, pointed Denis in the way he had to go, and then left him.

Denis walked along the corridor, checking the names on the doors, "Almoner", "Sister Theresa", "Sister Agatha", and "Mother Superior". He tried the handle on the door. As Astrid had said, it was unlocked. He went into the office and turned on the light. He looked in the cupboard, in the filing cabinet and in the desk, but his trousers were nowhere to be seen. He fought back the surge of panic which rose in him, turned off the light and went into Sister Agatha's room. He turned on the light and began to search there. After a minute or two he found them, neatly folded in the bottom drawer of the desk. "Thank God for that!" he said to himself, turned off the light and opened the door.

There, on the threshold, looking grim indeed stood the Mother Superior and Sister Agatha. With them was Police Constable John Banks wearing an expression that brooked no argument.

*

At Nutchester Police Station he was placed under arrest and formally charged on eight counts, including breaking and entering, theft, and assault. His own trousers had been retained as evidence and he had been provided with a pair of prison trousers in their place. He asked to see a solicitor, and the firm of Flint, Flint, & Flint sent the middle one to advise him. Upon seeing the charge list and hearing Denis's account of the events, he declined to represent Denis, and advised him to plead guilty and throw himself upon the mercy of the court.

*

Michael Spence waited for Denis in the hotel restaurant until half past eight and then asked the desk to phone his room. The clerk told him that Mr Foster had not checked in to confirm his reservation, and his luggage had been sent to the YMCA. Mr Spence phoned the YMCA and was told that the suitcase had been collected that very afternoon by a Mr Keith Brooks. He then phoned Keith who told him that Denis now had a suite reserved at the Belvedere. He phoned the Belvedere who told him that Mr Foster had booked a suite but had not checked in. Michael rang the Belvedere several times that evening, only to be told that Denis had still not appeared. At half past ten he phoned his wife who told him that Judy was in tears, Denis not having phoned her since leaving home the previous morning. He returned to Cranbury a very troubled man indeed.

*

The next morning Denis was taken from his cell and escorted to the Magistrates Court to be tried by Mr Middleton, the Stipendiary Magistrate. Inspector Groves led the prosecution for the police. He went through the charges against the accused: breaking and entering the convent; theft of a nun's habit; impersonating a nun in holy orders; obtaining money by false pretences, namely posing as a nun in order to collect money from passers-by; theft of a pair of trousers from a gentlemen's outfitters; offensive words and behaviour at the Imperial Hotel; assault on a porter at the Railway Hotel; and theft of money from the collecting tin. In support of his case he called a stream of witnesses, the hotel staff, the cabbies, the shop assistant and the nuns.

When the inspector concluded this litany of crime, Mr Middleton looked sharply at Denis.

"Well, young man, what have you got to say for yourself?"

It was fortunate for Denis that all Englishmen have an inherent sense of humour and an appreciation of the absurd. As he spun his tale of the events conspiring against him, the funnier aspects were not lost upon the magistrate. In time the corners of that worthy's mouth twitched and curled upwards involuntarily, the smile being removed physically but surreptitiously by a pass of the magistrate's hand. But Denis was a practised raconteur and knew from experience when he held an audience's attention. He sensed the changing atmosphere, and warming to his task, with an exaggeration here, a gloss there, here an embellishment, there a deletion, he spun out his story, punctuating it with pauses and gestures as the tale demanded. In time Mr Middleton gave up the pretence of concealing his smiles and soon permitted himself an occasional chuckle. As if absolved by this magisterial precedent, the ushers, the witnesses and the police then joined in. Denis sailed on gloriously and triumphantly, and when he had finished, though he did not receive or expect applause, he knew that no-one in the Courtroom was against him.

The magistrate's summing up was favourable.

He dismissed the breaking and entering charge on the grounds that Denis had entered the convent at the invitation of a resident.

He dismissed the charge of theft relating to the nun's habit as there was no intent permanently to deprive the nuns thereof. Denis had merely borrowed the garments – true, without consent, but then the nuns had his trousers without his consent, and exchange was no robbery.

He dismissed the charge of impersonation on the grounds that Denis had not at any time claimed to be a nun.

He dismissed the charge of obtaining money by false pretences on the grounds that the passers-by had deceived themselves. There was no evidence that Denis had asked them for money.

He dismissed the charge of stealing the trousers from the shop, on the grounds that it was imperfectly formed. The charge should have been obtaining by deceit, inasmuch as Denis had claimed that the convent had an account. Even that charge might have failed, Mr Middleton observed, as the prosecution had not bothered to present any evidence that the convent did *not* have an account at the gents' outfitters.

He dismissed the charges of offensive words and behaviour on the grounds that the complainants were only offended because they thought Denis was a nun which he clearly was not.

He dismissed the assault charge on the grounds that the attendant himself had assaulted Denis by gripping his arm and not releasing it when requested, behaviour which in itself might amount to false imprisonment.

With regard to the theft of the money from the collecting tin, the magistrate observed that the prosecution had not shown who the money had been stolen from. It could not have been stolen from the nuns, as the prosecution had been at pains to point out that Denis was *not* collecting for them. Nor could it have been stolen from those who had put it in the tin, as they had voluntarily abandoned possession of it. At worst it might constitute stealing by finding, but the charge had not been formed in those terms, and so must fail.

"However, Mr Foster," the magistrate concluded, "I do not wish you to think that the decision of this Court is an indication of a general leniency, or a disregard of the need to protect the rights and persons of our citizens. You have behaved foolishly and irresponsibly, leaving a trail of mayhem in your wake. I am therefore binding you over to keep the peace for six months. Any repetition of this sort of behaviour in that period will constitute a breach of my order and will be punishable by imprisonment."

He rapped the desk with his gavel and the Court rose.

Inspector Groves took Denis's arm. "Come with me, Mr Foster, and I will explain the conditions and draw up the necessary undertakings for you to sign. I need hardly tell you that I think that you are a very lucky young man indeed."

"I'll second that," said Denis truthfully. He left the court thanking his lucky stars, but that luck ran out the moment he opened the front door of his house in Cranbury.

* * *

THE MAJOR

It was Quiz Night at the Red Lion. Five teams of four were taking part. The last question had been put and the teams exchanged their sheets of answers in order for them to be marked. Ron Baker repeated the questions in turn and called out the correct answers. Each team marked the sheet of an opponent and noted the total of correct answers on the bottom. The papers were then passed to Ron for adjudication.

"Well, this is interesting," said Ron. "We have a tie. Teams two and four have each got twenty-one correct answers out of the twenty-five. So it is tie-break time. I'm going to ask those two teams one question and as it is a tie-break that question will not be as easy as the last ones were. Right, pens and paper at the ready. Here's the question. Who was appointed to take over the command of the Eighth Army after General Aukinleck was dismissed? If you think you know the answer write it down."

The members of team two were Henry and Betty Lambton and Bob and Helen Wetherby, while the members of team four were the vicar, the Rev. Claud Higgins, Alf and Audrey Wagstaff and Major Ian Brodie. As the question was called out team two smiled at such an easy question and wrote down their answer, 'General Montgomery'. Three members of team four would have done the same, but the Major put a cautionary finger to his lips, quietly took the pencil from the vicar and wrote down 'General William (Strafer) Gott'.

"All done?" asked Ron. "Right, pass up your answers." He looked at the two sheets of paper and made his announcement. "The winners are team four. They gave the correct answer which was 'General Gott'. Congratulations team four!"

"No! It was Monty," cried Henry Lambton. "Everybody knows that."

"Henry, I told you the tie-break question wasn't going to be as easy as the others. Well done, team four. I suppose the Major being an Army man helped, didn't it?"

"Well, I was there at the time when Strafer Gott was shot down on his way to take up his command," replied the Major.

"That's not fair!" shouted Henry Lambton. "He knew the answer!" Laughter filled the Red Lion at this banal remark, but Henry plunged on. "He was there, so he obviously knew the answer."

"Quizzes are to find out what you know, Henry," said Ron, "however you acquired that knowledge."

"Yeah, but that was an easy question for him because he already knew the answer."

Laughter broke out once again, and Ron felt obliged to soothe Henry's hurt feelings. "Suppose the question had been about cuts of meat, Henry, would that have been unfair?"

"That's different," mumbled Henry, picking up his glass.

The quiz over, the pub patrons resumed their normal conversation. "So you were in North Africa, were you, during the war?" asked the vicar.

"For quite a while, but I also saw action in Europe. But Henry was right. That was an easy question for me. Our adjutant, John Wood, was related to Strafer Gott, or led us to believe he was, which is quite a different thing. He never specifically made that claim, but he never corrected anyone who made that assumption. What a shit that man was, an arsehole crawler of the first water!"

The vicar rose from his chair. "I think I'd better join Joyce at her table," he tactfully said. "I've neglected her long enough." He left and his place was taken by Ron.

"You didn't like him, then?" Ron asked.

"I loathed him! We were at Sandhurst together and clashed frequently. He had absolutely no idea of how to command men. In '39 we were in our barracks being fitted out for overseas duty. He was the adjutant and one day he marched a private over to one of my sergeants. 'Put this man on a charge, sergeant!' he ordered. 'Yes sir. What is the charge?' 'Gross insolence!' 'In what way, sir?' 'He farted as I was walking past!' 'Farting's not against King's Regulations, sir,' said my sergeant. 'We all have to do it now and again.' 'I said *gross* insolence, sergeant. Add to the charge, 'by raising his right leg and shaking it vigorously''. How my sergeant prevented himself from laughing I'll never know. Anyway he stood his ground and said, 'I'm afraid that's not a chargeable offence, sir,' he said. 'Are you refusing to obey an order, sergeant?' 'In my opinion, sir, that's not a lawful command.' Full marks to the sergeant, but the adjutant marched him before the C.O. As he was one of my sergeants I was called in and supported him. The C.O. said, 'For God's sake! Enough of this bloody nonsense! We've got a war to win, so forget it!' The adjutant had to accept the old man's decision but he took it out on that sergeant's squad. He landed them with every shitty job he could and restricted their privileges as much as possible."

The Major stopped talking and took another swig of his beer, but his memories coursed on. "You know, you must never push your men too far. The adjutant had a well-groomed military moustache. It was his pride and joy. He used to wax it! One night as he left the Mess he was grabbed by strong arms. A torch was shone in his face so that he couldn't see who his attackers were and he was led to the Other Ranks ablutions. He was held down in a chair struggling until a voice said, "This is a cut-throat razor so keep very still!" He kept still and remained so as one side of his moustache was shaved off. That done, his attackers fled. You can imagine the horror when he got back to his room and saw what they had done, but he had no choice but to shave off the other half. Do you know, he looked most unimpressive without that moustache. It emphasised his very weak chin. It goes without saying that he went to the C.O. the next morning and put in a complaint against my sergeant's squad. I was called in again. 'What makes you think it was the men of this particular squad?' the C.O. asked the adjutant. 'I just know it, sir,' he replied. So I supplied my own answer and said, 'Perhaps it's because they are fed up with being given every shitty job going and have had their entitlements reduced to the minimum!' The old man was furious. He was no fool and was aware of the adjutant's character defects. 'Look!' he cried, 'There's a bloody war on and I need every good man I've got. Our men are hard, John, very hard. We have trained them that way. We've trained them to kill, and I'd rather they killed the enemy than one of my own officers. You've lost your moustache, but it could have been much worse. I don't want to find you've lost your testicles next time. Now get back to your duties. We'll be getting our orders any day now and I want the men in full fighting fettle.' So the adjutant just had to leave it at that, but whether he had learnt anything, I doubt."

"I can see why you didn't like him, Major," said Ron. "But when he was in North Africa with you was he any different?"

"You can't put on airs and graces in a battle situation, Ron, so he had to change somewhat, but he was still a prick. After we had finished in North Africa and returned home for D Day, the old man took the opportunity to find him a desk job in Cairo so we left him there and I haven't seen or heard of him since."

"What about your C.O.? Is he still around? Do you ever see him?"

The Major smiled. "Yes, Ron," he replied. "I see him now and again. And so do you. His name is Colonel Buckmaster."

"Colonel Buck….. You mean our Squire?"

"That's right, Ron. The Squire is my old C.O."

*

Ian Brodie was tall, tanned and athletic. He was born in 1911, the son of an Army Captain who served throughout the First World War and who, through his experiences of those four grim years, taught his son the true character of men. "Look out for fools in high places," he told him. "You will find them in all walks of life. They are a canker on society. They are like eunuchs – incapable of producing anything themselves, they see their duty as preventing others who can – and just like eunuchs they have no balls. This makes them crafty and vicious, so watch out if you come up against any of them. They're easy to recognize once you know what to look for. Put your trust in good honest ordinary men, Ian. They won't let you down as long as you are honest with them."

After graduating from Oxford, where he was an enthusiastic member of the University Officer Training Corps, he joined the regular army and went to Sandhurst as a cadet where he met the eunuch-in-the-making, John Wood. His father had been right. You can spot them immediately, once you recognize the signs. At Sandhurst Ian was awarded the Sword of Honour for being the most promising cadet of the course, much to the bitter chagrin of John Wood. From Sandhurst he joined the 1st Dragoons and served with distinction throughout the Second World War in North Africa and Europe, coming out unscathed. After returning from the Korean conflict he left the Army as a Major, after twenty-one years of service, to enjoy a carefree bachelor life in Nutcombe, living comfortably on his inheritance and Army pension.

*

A few weeks had elapsed since that quiz night and the Major made his way into the Red Lion for his normal evening's drinks and conversation. He picked up the Nutchester Chronicle from one of the tables and scanned through the pages unhurriedly. Seeing one page he let out a cry. "Bloody hell! I can't believe it!"

"What's that, Major?" asked Ron.

"You know that chap I told you about a few weeks ago, that shit-bag, John Wood? Well he's only an MP! He's a minister in Churchill's new set-up. Look, here's a photograph of him. Well, bugger me!"

"But why is he in the Chronicle? He's not an MP from round here, is he?"

"You're not going to believe this, Ron, but it's just been announced that he's the chap who is going to officially open the Nutt Valley By-Pass in six weeks' time."

"That's nice for you, Major," joked Ron. "You'll be able to shake hands and talk about old times again."

"It's no joke, Ron. That eunuch's on his way to the top! He could become the Prime Minister one day!"

This thought preyed upon his mind over the coming days as he wondered whether it could conceivably be prevented.

*

For more than a year contractors had been hard at work completing the last section of a by-pass which would greatly reduce the traffic passing through the villages. The final section would join up with the already completed work at a newly constructed junction a mile from the centre of Nutcombe. In preparation for the official opening the County Council had spent time and money to ensure its success. On one side of the new junction was the site where the contractors' heavy plant and equipment had been positioned, while on the other side the workmen's cabins had been housed. These two areas had now been cleared and a dais for the great and the good had been erected at the best vantage point. A loudspeaker system had been installed for the speeches which were expected to be many. The Nutcombe & District Silver Band had been invited to perform at the opening ceremony and the schools had been encouraged to take part with song and dance. At the Minister's request a section on one side of the junction had been earmarked for the BBC cameras, the Press and foreign journalists, for he considered it important enough for the event to be recorded for posterity and for his own publicity. A temporary slip road had been created so that a cavalcade of official cars could progress along the new stretch of road as soon as the ribbon had been cut, and police had been put on alert to control the hundreds of onlookers which were expected.

    The day of the grand opening arrived. The dignitaries were seated under the canopy of the dais – the Lord Lieutenant, the Bishop, the Mayor and County Councillors, the Squire and, in the centre of the first row, the Minister, John Wood. The scene was one of colour as the uniforms of the St John Ambulance Brigade, the Scouts and Guides, the Silver Band and the schoolchildren all blended in haphazard harmony. Inside the ropes which marked the limit of where the public could stand were three mounted policemen, and no-one thought it unusual when a mounted officer of the Household Cavalry in full uniform eased his way between the police horses. He sat tall in the saddle with bronze and scarlet-plumed helmet gleaming, and with his white belt and sash dazzling in the sun. Upon his chest hung two gallantry and four campaign medals, three of them with oak-leaf clasps. He held the reins of his horse with his left hand, and in his right he carried his Sword of Honour unsheathed and held upright against his shoulder. He was a magnificent sight; for the rider, Major Ian Brodie, had taken trouble to see that it was so. He wanted the photographic record to show him at his best.

After the speeches, the schoolchildren's song and dance performance and the Silver Band's stirring marches, the serious aspect of the ceremony took centre stage. The Bishop rose and said a prayer. The Town Clerk walked to the ribbon, carrying the velvet-lined case containing the ceremonial scissors and held it open ready for the Minister to take them to cut the ribbon. John Wood rose from his seat, walked down the steps and made his way forward. At this moment the Major dug his heels into the charger which set off at speed past the dais towards the ribbon stretched across the road. He brought his sword arm down and as the charger breasted the tape he leant back and slashed the ribbon through. Master horseman that he was, he brought the horse to a standstill, reared it up on its hind legs and turned it about to face the onlookers. With sword raised high he shouted, "I declare this by-pass officially opened. God save the Queen!" With that he sheathed his sword and led the horse briskly towards the cheering and clapping crowd which parted to let him through. As he passed the dais the Minister saw for the first time who the horseman was, and his face turned thunder-cloud blue, bizarrely flecked with patches of purple as the Major continued his leisurely way back to the Squire's stables with a satisfied smile upon his face.

Meanwhile, the driver of the first official car on the slip road, assuming that there had been a change of plan and that the by-pass was now officially opened, started his engine and set off along the by-pass followed quickly by the other cars in the cavalcade. The dignitaries on the dais looked at each other in puzzlement, realizing that the officially-planned ceremony now had to be aborted, and eventually and slowly they made their way through the crowd and back to their waiting cars. All this was filmed by the BBC cameras for the evening TV transmission and by the local and foreign press photographers.

*

A few days later Peter Penny entered the Red Lion for his lunch and was greeted by the Major.

"Peter, come and join me here. I want to talk to you. Ron, a pint for Peter, if you please."

The blacksmith sat down in the proffered seat. "That's kind of you, Major. What is it you want to talk to me about?"

"Peter," he began, "I'm told you're a dab hand when it comes to legal matters. You may know that the week before last I made a fool of myself at the by-pass ceremony."

"Yes, I was there, but I wouldn't say you made a fool of yourself. It was more entertaining than some politician spouting his usual pious nonsense."

"That's nice of you to say so, Peter, but I fear the Law takes a less tolerant attitude. Soon after that event I was paid a visit by Inspector Groves. He told me he was arresting me on suspicion of committing various offences. He cautioned me and took me off to the police station . He had a search warrant and took away my sword as evidence. I was released on bail but yesterday I was formally charged and summoned to appear at a preliminary hearing at the Magistrates Court in Nutchester a couple of weeks hence."

"What exactly were you charged with?"

"What wasn't I? Criminal damage, insulting behaviour, criminal trespass, endangering the public and various public order offences."

"That's ridiculous! You didn't do any of those things. They're throwing the book at you for no reason"

"Oh, they have a reason, Peter, believe me. This is all inspired by the Minister, John Wood. He hates my guts."

"Oh, I see. That's the bloke you were talking to Ron about at that quiz night."

"That's the fellah. He's in the big league, so if he *is* behind this I'm out of my depth. I'm playing poker with someone who has far more chips than I've got. I knew I needed legal advice so I went to Flints and saw the middle one. He couldn't help me as he is acting for the police. Then I went to Warrenders but they said that they couldn't either as it would raise a conflict of interest."

"In what way?"

"They didn't say. Anyway, I was telling Ron here and he said I should have come to you in the first place, so here I am asking for your help."

The blacksmith took a sip from his pint mug and sat deep in thought. He always felt honoured when someone sought his advice on legal matters, but this seemed a case well beyond his ability; and if a Minister of the Crown was pulling the strings what hope had he of succeeding? More than that, there was something very determined about the Major's actions.

"Tell me, Major," he asked. "Your performance at the by-pass seemed very deliberate and predetermined. It was no spontaneous affair. You must have thought long and hard about it. You were in full uniform and mounted upon one of the Squire's chargers which I recognized at once. I can understand why you felt the need to provoke the Minister, but why in that fashion?"

The major laughed. "I didn't need to think it up, Peter. It was designed for me. I was at Sandhurst in 1932 and one evening when we were in the mess one of the cadets read out a Times Newspaper report from Australia. It seemed that an Irishman named Francis de Groot, a major in the 15th Hussars, had a grudge against the Australian Prime Minister, Joseph Lyons, and wished to embarrass him. He chose as the appropriate occasion the official opening of the Sydney Harbour Bridge. As the Prime Minister was about to cut the ribbon and formally open the bridge, Francis de Groot rode forward on his horse, drew his ceremonial sword, slashed through the ribbon and declared the bridge open. Well, when the cadet read out that report we all hooted with laughter and someone proposed a toast to Francis de Groot. But one cadet refused to join in the toast. You've guessed it - John Wood. He said Francis de Groot should be court-martialled and thrown out of the Hussars."

He paused to take a swig from his glass then continued. "After I had read in the Chronicle that John Wood was to open the by-pass the similarities flooded into my mind. Francis de Groot had a grudge against a politician. He wished to humiliate him as he was about to perform a very public opening ceremony. He was a cavalry officer with a ceremonial sword.

When I realised how well those facts fitted my own position I knew that I had no better choice. Add to that the delicious irony of repeating Francis de Groot's actions in front of and upon the cadet who thought he should be court-martialled, well, it was obvious, wasn't it?"

Although the Major was chuckling at his recollections, Peter Penny was serious. "Is the satisfaction of re-enacting that feat sufficient to counter a fine or a jail sentence?" he asked.

The smile left the Major's face. "I'm beginning to doubt that now, Peter," he said, "but I'm hoping with your help I'll get off scot-free. The question is, do you think you can help me, and if so, will you?"

"I honestly think that this is beyond me, Major. You did not just embarrass the Minister, you humiliated him. If he *is* behind your prosecution he will seek to inflict the same public humiliation upon you. He will seek the maximum publicity, so it is not at the Quarter Sessions in Nutchester you will appear but at the Old Bailey. And frankly, Major, that's a non-starter for me."

"Yeah, you're right. I'm up the creek without a paddle then, aren't I?"

"I'm afraid so." The blacksmith paused. "Unless..."

"Unless what, Peter?"

"Let me think. Let me think. You said that the police have instructed Ephraim Flint. I know him. I've come up against him a couple of times. He is not the brightest briquette in the brazier, so if we can outwit him at the preliminary hearing and have the case thrown out, there will be no trial. Yes, I can see how that can be done."

The Major was heartened by Peter's use of the first person plural pronoun. "So what do we do?" he asked.

"We have got to take Flint's eye off the ball, let him think there is no opposition. You must appear to the world an already defeated man. If anyone asks, say you know you've been a fool, will apologize, plead guilty and hope the Courts will deal leniently with you. Act as if you have accepted the inevitable."

"And what will you do?" asked the Major.

"Just leave everything to me."

*

Over the next few days Peter visited the Squire to examine his horses' hooves and took the opportunity to raise one or two other matters. He visited the vicarage and spoke to the vicar and his wife, Joyce, about the wrought-iron work in and around the church and the churchyard, taking the opportunity to raise one or two other matters. He called in on Miss Betty at her corner shop and told her in strictest confidence that the Major had told him that he accepted that he is on a hiding to nothing and hoped his good service record will get him off with a light sentence at the Quarter Sessions. He said that, as he had been told this in the strictest confidence, Betty must keep that knowledge to herself. As Peter expected, soon the whole village sympathized with the Major in his hopeless plight.

He visited Nutchester on a couple of days. He went to the Chronicle offices and spoke to the photographers in the News Department. He went to the County Council offices and spoke to the people in the Roads and Highways Department. He went to the County Library spending hours among the law books. He had been there before but now his task was different.

Previously he had been searching for loopholes and quirks in the law, but now he needed the law to support him.

By the time of the preliminary hearing his strategy was clear in his mind, and he relished the coming fray.

*

The hearing was held with Mr Montague Middleton, Stipendiary Magistrate, presiding. The Major pleaded 'not guilty' to all the charges, which surprised Mr Flint as he had been assured by all and sundry that the Major would plead guilty. Inspector Groves then gave formal evidence of the circumstances relating to the charges and of the Major's arrest.

"Have you any questions you would like to put to the Inspector, Mr Penny?" the magistrate asked.

"Yes, thank you, your honour. Inspector, in drawing up these charges, were you subjected to any political pressure?"

"In what way do you mean?"

"Specifically, has the Minister, Mr John Wood, played any part in the process?"

"Certainly not."

"So the Minister has not contacted you or been in touch with you at any stage?"

"That is correct."

Sitting next to Peter, the Major took out his pen and put a tick against 'item 1' in his notebook.

"Inspector, I take it you will be calling upon witnesses in support of your evidence?"

"No, not at this stage."

"Why ever not?"

"There's no need at this stage. It is an open and shut case after all."

Mr Middleton's lips tightened, but it was the blacksmith who spoke.

"Sorry, Inspector. Would you please repeat your last sentence?"

Inspector Groves knew he had made a grave mistake and sought to limit the damage it had caused. "What I meant to say was that I had in mind not wasting the Court's time in matters that could be taken for granted."

Far from limiting the damage, the Inspector had compounded it, but Peter did not seek to pursue his advantage. Instead he pressed on with his questioning. "So, if no other prosecution witnesses are to be called I must look to you to answer all my questions."

"I don't think I'll be able to answer all of them."

"Again, why ever not? This is a police prosecution led by you. You interviewed the defendant, you made the arrest, you served the warrant, and you signed the charge sheet. If you cannot answer my questions, who can?"

At this point Mr Ephraim Flint rose to speak. "Your honour, I request that this case be adjourned for a week or two. It seems my staff may have been delinquent in preparing the prosecution case and justice cannot properly be served when one side is so disadvantaged."

Mr Middleton addressed Peter. "Well, Mr Penny. What observation do you have to Mr Flint's request?"

"We could not possibly agree, your honour. It is the duty of both sides to prepare their case at all stages of the proceedings, and justice would certainly not be served if one party were absolved of their incompetence at the expense of the other, more competent party."

"I'm inclined to agree," said the magistrate. "Application refused. Carry on, Mr Penny."

The Inspector's mistake was telling against the prosecution, and the Major ticked 'item 2' as Peter continued.

"Thank you, your honour. Inspector, the first charge relates to damage of property. Could you tell the Court what property and what damage?"

"It was the ribbon across the road. The defendant cut it with his sword."

The laughter was heard beyond the courtroom and the Inspector began fingering his collar. Mr Flint sat dismayed, viewing the floor at his feet.

"But the ribbon was there to be cut, wasn't it?"

"Yes, but not by him. It was there to be cut by the person who would then declare the by-pass officially opened."

"But at the beginning of this hearing did you not state that that was precisely what my client had done? He cut the ribbon and declared the by-pass opened."

"Yes, but he shouldn't have done. It was the Minister who should have done it."

"Is protocol then a police matter, Inspector?"

The inspector did not answer, and the Major ticked 'item 3'. Peter pressed on. "Trespass is a civil offence, but you have charged my client with criminal trespass. Can you tell the Court what that involves?"

"The defendant entered upon Crown Property without due authorisation."

"I take it the Crown Property in question is the section of road completing the by-pass. Is that correct?" He turned towards the magistrate. "I have here a copy, your honour, which I now pass to you, of that section of the building contract covering this very point. Before the opening ceremony the property was vested in the contractors, but once the by-pass was declared open it passed immediately to the Crown as a public highway. No criminal trespass is therefore involved. My client was allowed, as all member of the public were, to travel along that public highway."

Mr Middleton was handed the copy and began studying it.

"But the by-pass wasn't opened!" protested the Inspector.

"Really?" said Peter. "I've seen it full of traffic every day for the past two or three weeks."

The Major ticked 'item 4'.

Mr Flint rose again. "Your honour, I feel I must again request an adjournment. We are ill-prepared."

"Application refused!" said Mr Middleton. "Carry on, Mr Penny."

"Now, Inspector, I'd like to turn to the charge of insulting behaviour. It is not alleged that my client used any threatening, abusive or insulting words, so the question I would like you to answer is, to whom was his behaviour insulting, the public in general or one particular individual?"

"Both."

"How many complaints have you received from the general public?"

"Well, none actually."

"And from an individual?"

The Inspector glanced across at Mr Flint who gave a slight shake of his head. "None," he admitted, "though I can imagine the Minister was very put out."

"Putting out a Minister is not yet a criminal offence," said the blacksmith, and the Major ticked 'item 5'.

Peter continued. "Let me pass on to the charge of endangering the public. Would you please tell the court exactly how the public were endangered?"

"The defendant charged along the road brandishing his sword. There were hundreds of people in the vicinity."

The blacksmith turned towards the magistrate. "Your honour, I have here several photographs taken by the Nutchester Chronicle's news team detailing the sequence of my client's actions upon horseback. In none of them can one see any brandishing of his sword near any member of the public." He passed them to Mr Middleton who studied each one in turn.

"Thank you, Mr Penny. Please proceed."

The Major ticked 'item 6', screwed the top back onto his fountainpen and replaced it in his pocket. He could see the job was almost done, just awaiting the killer blow.

"Which brings me to the sword, Inspector. You seized it under the powers of the search warrant. My question is, why?"

Here Mr Flint jumped to his feet again. "Your honour, this is grossly unfair. Mr Penny is just fishing for any matter to bolster his case. He is taking unfair advantage of our failure to adequately prepare our case."

"I will concede that he is taking advantage of your lapse," said the magistrate, "but I see nothing unfair about it. Furthermore, Mr Flint, the question of whether a matter is grossly unfair rests with this Bench and not with you. Kindly proceed, Mr Penny."

"Thank you, your honour. Inspector, I asked you why you seized my client's sword."

"Well, for evidence, of course."

"But I do not see that evidence in court. You have not produced it as an exhibit. Why is that?"

The Inspector turned to face Mr Flint, his appealing look craving support and assistance, but Mr Flint sat slumped and resigned with his eyes closed. In his mind he had already conceded defeat.

Mr Middleton had sat as a magistrate for many years, and recognized the body-language of duplicity.

"You seem to have difficulty in answering that question, Inspector, so I will ask you a very simple one. Can you produce the sword?"

"No, your honour."

"Why is that?"

"It is in London, your honour. The Minister asked for it to be sent to him."

There was a gasp around the court as the full implication set in. The look on the magistrate's face was thunderous.

"Inspector," he said sternly, "I have to warn you that your position is precarious in the extreme. You stated on oath that no political pressure had been brought to bear on you, and that the Minister had not contacted you. You also stated that the sword had been seized as evidence, yet sending it to an individual is incompatible with that statement. Unless Mr Penny has any more questions for you, you may for the moment stand down."

"No more questions, your honour, but if it pleases the Court I could call the Bishop of Nutchester, the Right Reverent Dr Robert Swineforth, and the Squire of Nutcombe, Colonel Buckmaster, to provide character evidence on behalf of my client. The Squire is particularly well placed, since he was the Commanding Officer of both my client and Mr John Wood and would happily give evidence as to the fine character of the former." The stress he placed upon those words carried the clear indication that the Squire would in no way do that for the Minister.

"There is no need, Mr Penny. I have already made my decision. I find the charges brought against Major Brodie completely without foundation and the case against him is therefore dismissed. I find this whole matter has very disturbing aspects and I shall be writing reports for submission to the appropriate authorities in the coming days."

*

It was noon when Peter and the Major were driven back to Nutcombe by the Squire in his Rolls. "I rather fancy the Minister's train has hit the buffers, don't you, Ian?" the Squire asked the Major as they made their way. "And as for you, Penny, you've obviously got hidden depths – hang on, they can't be both obvious *and* hidden, can they? Anyway, I suppose you'll be upping your farriery charges now, eh?"

"I've never thought of having to, Squire. I've always relied upon your good judgement to see when and by how much my services require upward adjustment."

"You crafty old fox. Anyway, well done, Penny."

"I didn't mean to ruin the Inspector, though," the blacksmith continued. "That was a complete surprise. I feel sorry for him."

"Don't be! He was a rotten apple in the barrel."

"I don't think he was rotten as much as weak," said the Major. "He should have stood up to John Wood just as my sergeant did. Do you remember, Sir?"

"What, the farting incident, you mean? 'Raised his right leg and shook it vigorously'! What bloody nonsense! That characterises the man."

They drew up outside Peter's forge at two o'clock. As Peter got out, the Major said, "Peter, I'd like to buy you a drink this evening. Shall we say seven in the Red Lion? Bring Mrs Penny along too. Will you be there? Good man!"

*

At seven o'clock on that balmy late June evening Peter and his Nutcombe wife, Peggy, left their cottage and walked the short distance to the pub, where Ron's wife, Betty, stood watching by the entrance. As they neared it Betty ran inside calling, "They're coming! They're coming!" The people in the Red Lion became silent until Peter and his wife entered. Then the song rang out. "For he's a jolly good fellow!" The villagers would have borne him aloft on their shoulders if there had been two men strong enough to lift the gentle giant up. It seemed the whole village was there, in the pub itself and in the beer-garden where Ron had put out bunting around the picnic tables. Peter looked around stunned. He had expected a couple of quiet drinks with the Major – nothing more – but now it seemed most of the village was in the pub to greet him. Peter's other wives rushed forward to greet him. Leonard Bradshaw the proprietor of the Shire Bus and Coach Company had sent a minibus to pick them up from their villages and to take them back home later, all at his own expense.

Hermione Pollifax, the Squire's weird niece, came into the pub with Eustacia Crabbe. They looked around to see who else was there. Audrey Wagstaff spotted them and called out, "If you're looking for Princess Moolaaba, she's behind the bar with the rest of the spirits."

"Bitch!" hissed Hermione between gritted teeth.

Ron noticed Billy Enright coming into the pub. "Sorry, Billy," he said. "You're too young to be in the bar."

"It's all right, Mr Baker," responded Joyce, the vicar's wife. "He is with me, and we're just making our way through to the beer-garden."

Amos Lovejoy approached Eric. "Look, lad," he pleaded, "do me a favour and see Mrs Lovejoy gets home straight away, only she's not feeling very well."

"No! Why should I? I'm here to enjoy myself."

"Two and six on your wages if you do it," the undertaker offered.

"Five bob and it's yours," countered Eric.

"All right, you greedy little beggar," agreed a reluctant Lovejoy, and he watched Eric lead Arabella away. "And to think people believe he is simple!"

Fred Atkins from the garage put his empty glass on the bar counter. "Fill her up again, Ron," he said. "That's a right lovely ale, is that."

"I'm glad you like it," said Ron, working the pump. "I think it's because I'm watering the beer only with full-strength water these days!" The regulars roared with laughter.

The blacksmith made his way through the crowd acknowledging the smiles, the handshakes and the pats on the back. He passed Daisy Dimple and gave her a friendly wink.

"Is there something going on between you two?" asked Eugenie Lascelles.

"I'll keep that little secret to myself if you don't mind," answered Daisy.

"I only asked," continued Eugenie, "because I notice you've got a new wrought-iron gate in front of your cottage."

At nine o'clock PC John Banks drew up in the police car and sought out the Major. "I've got something for you, sir," he said, and handed the Major his Sword of Honour. "With the compliments of Mr Middleton. He phoned the Solicitor General immediately after the hearing and demanded it be returned at once."

"Well, I'll be damned!" was all that the Major could say in a husky voice.

"And I've got a letter for you, Peter," the PC continued. "Again from Mr Middleton."

Peter opened the letter and read,

"Dear Mr Penny,

I am retiring at the end of this term and it should give me much pleasure if you would join me at a small private function I am giving in mid-July. I do hope you will be able to come.

Yours very sincerely,

Montague Middleton."

The blacksmith read the letter twice and smiled. "What a perfect gentleman the Magistrate is," he said, "but behind this invitation lies his subtle warning that the new Stipendiary Magistrate could be a very different kettle of fish, so you'd better quit while you're ahead, Peter Penny!"

* * *

[Note: The Sidney Harbour Bridge incident is factual.]

About the Author:

Ken Kelsey is a Barrister living in Dorking, Surrey. He has written three books of Number Puzzles, published together by Dorset Press as a single volume, 'The Ultimate Book of Number Puzzles' and a book of humorous poems, 'They Could Be Verse'. The present book brings together his sense of humour, his knowledge of the Law and his love of poetry.

Printed in Great Britain
by Amazon